ACTION

MIND

D.A

WAKE UP

BODY

.P.

REFLECTION

REACTION

I Am Responsible For My Own Life

The day-to-day positive living model

by Fergus Barrett

I Am Responsible For My Own Life

ISBN Soft Back Edition: 978-1-911180-44-9
ISBN Hard Back Edition: 978-1-911180-50-0

Printed in Ireland by Lettertec

Self Contract

- I am fully committed to making positive changes in my life
- I will do my very best to carry out everything in my daily action plan (DAP)
- I will view all obstacles in my way as opportunities
- I will hold myself accountable for everything I do and don't do
- I will not make or tolerate excuses
- I will live each day to the best of my ability
- I am responsible for my own life

Signed: ....

Contents

Chapter 1

Introduction – One Life, Live It

Success doesn't choose you, you choose success.

This is a book of very simple ideas and techniques to help you achieve happiness.

When you wake up in the morning you start a whole new day. You do this in the knowledge that you have the mental and physical capability to do whatever you want to do.

Planning out your day using a Daily Action Plan (DAP) will help you to move through the day with confidence, hope, motivation and determination.

Each day you can achieve success by setting daily goals. By living in accordance with your values and beliefs you will live an authentic life.

When you put structure into your day you make the decision to take back control of your life. You decide that you will live each day to the best of your ability.

You need to remember one very important thing: when you live an authentic life, you not only owe it to yourself, but to all your family and friends as well.

You are not being selfish by paying attention to yourself. You deserve this. When you live a happy and contented life, your family and friends will all be over the moon for you. No family member or friend wants to see you unhappy, unwell or disillusioned. So you see, it's in everyone's interest that you live a fulfilling and rewarding life. People want to be around happy, motivated and inspiring people.

Now you might say that surely not every day is going to be rosy. And yes, you are right. You are never going to get 10 out of 10 every single day. But it shouldn't stop you from striving towards it. Some days will be an 8, some a 3. But if your day is a 6, it's still better than a 5, 4, 3, 2 or 1.

Learn from each day. Learn from each setback. Nobody is saying it's going to be easy; it won't be. But you can decide if you are going to raise the Blue Peter flag (see Chapter 2) and head out to sea, or stay in the safety of the harbour.

This book is my way of helping you to structure your daily life and to help you understand how important your values, beliefs and life balance are for you. Your Daily Action Plan should contain everything you intend to do on a given day. You can use the six steps of the DAP to stay focused and on track to achieving all your goals.

When you open your eyes first thing in the morning and you realise you are alive and well, you are in a position that millions of people around the world would love to be in. Think about that ... instead of envying others what they have, there are millions of people around this planet who would love to have what you have.

We have become accustomed to believing that we will not be happy until we look like the people on TV and in magazines and have the same amount of material wealth as them. It's all a lie … *you* can decide when you should be happy.

Open your eyes to the world. Take time to distinguish fact from fiction, truth from lies, and life's reality from commercial illusion.

I heard a great phrase once: people need to walk around each day in a 'live awake mode'.

You can spend the rest of your life going through the motions, day after day after day. Or, you can decide now that you are going to take action. You are going to take your life back. You are going to live to your full potential.

Every day we are attacked on all fronts, in the newspapers, on the television, in magazines, billboards, social media, etc. We are told we need Product A to live better lives, that if we wear Product B we will be better people, if we eat Product C we will be healthier, if we drive Product D we will be happier.

It's my opinion that we are surrendering the logical part of our brain to our emotions. We are letting our emotions dictate our lives. We are mentally weaker than the generations gone before us. Our emotions are running our lives. We need this, we must have that. We eat unhealthy food because we are stressed, which makes us depressed because we are now putting on weight. We don't train because we are overweight so we get more depressed.

Our resilience is low. Our ability to use logic is being overridden by our emotions.

I know I don't need a burger and chips but I want them anyway. Why did I eat them – I wasn't even hungry. Now I'm depressed.

With so much food being produced in the world, it has become very cheap to eat rubbish. It's so convenient – it's there in our faces at the checkout. Again, we are being attacked on all fronts.

I only went in to pay for petrol and ended up with a latte and two bars of chocolate … they were on special offer.

We are mentally weaker than in years gone by and we need to toughen up.

Example

You are in a room full of free food. Ask yourself: do you eat all you can eat or do you eat just enough to satisfy your hunger? How many people would say that they ate themselves silly? The logical part of the brain switches off and our emotions go wild. What is happening to our self-control? Why aren't we mentally stronger? At the end of the day, it's ourselves we are doing it to. And then you feel guilty for doing it. I had better go and train to help reverse the damage.

How many people work out to keep the weight off because they are eating some rubbish food? I know I do at times. Isn't it mad? You eat rubbish food and then you train to prevent putting on weight from the extra calories. Even though we know that a healthy fit body is 80 per cent food and 20 per cent exercise (see page 43), and yet we still do this.

We need to stop and look around and say enough is enough.

I'm not going to be coerced and manipulated into believing I need so many material things.

Isn't it time we all opened our eyes and realised that nobody actually cares about our health and well-being. They only want us to spend our money.

It's only when we wake up and see what is going on – see how we are being manipulated into believing we need all this rubbish food and shiny items – that we can live a life using logic rather than emotions.

By planning your day, by putting structure into your day, you can decide to say no. Enough is enough. I'm taking back control.

I'll buy only what I actually need. I'll eat only when I'm actually hungry. I'll put only healthy food into my body. I'll decide that by changing my diet from processed food to actual real food it will help stop many of those health problems I have. It may even lead me to taking fewer medications.

We need to toughen up mentally. We need to reflect on and review each day. Where can we improve? What worked? What didn't? How can we improve for the next day?

I'm not saying you have to give up all the little treats in life. Everything in moderation. If you don't make the necessary changes, you will still be sitting at home on your couch watching the TV soaps and feeling depressed. Feeling good for nothing. No motivation, no drive, no focus. It doesn't matter which car you drive or how expensive your clothes are: if your belly is bulging out and you can't walk 100 metres without sweating, you will not feel healthy and happy.

Look at all the happy, professional and healthy people you know. Do they eat healthily? Do they train? Do they get up early and put a structure on their day? My money says they do.

Oh, why can't I be like them?

You can be!

- Get up early
- Eat more healthily
- Do some exercise
- Set some goals
- Be positive
- Stay focused
- Reflect on your day

There is no magic to this. If you have time to sit and watch TV every day, you have time to spend making your life healthier and happier.

No excuses.

Ask yourself: why are all these so-called professionals trying to sell me this idea? Is it really that good? Do I actually need it?

Remember, the person that knows you best is *you*.

You know what you need to do. Whenever you are unsure, all you have to do is take a minute. Ask yourself what is best for me in this situation. Do I need this? Do I need to do this?

Listen to your own answers. Be careful of what your emotions are saying ... use your brain. Think logically. Be strong.

Instead:

- Eat some healthy food
- Do some physical exercise a few times a week
- Control your emotions
- Think about it before you do it
- Ask yourself, is this good for me or not?
- Bring some clarity into your life
- Don't be fooled by the big companies and the media

Success isn't about a car, clothes, house, etc. Success is when you are happy in your own skin. Happy living a loving life in your own home. Success is when you wake up in the morning and you're grateful for being healthy and having the ability to do whatever you put your mind to.

No matter how much money you have in the bank, no matter what you drive, or how good your health insurance is, if you can't kick a ball around with your children, run a kilometre, fit into your trousers, live without medication for this, that and the other, it all means nothing in the game of life. The person with the healthy, happy, loving family will end up being the winner.

Strive to do your best. If some days are a 6 out of 10, well it's still better than a 4, 2 or 0. Do your best. When you are reflecting back on the day, figure out how you can do better.

Remember**...live awake.**

It's very simple: you have one life – live it!

Chapter 2
The Positive Living Model

We cannot direct the wind, but we can adjust the sails

Anonymous

That New Year's Feeling

Ever start a new exercise regime, only to let it fade away again? Or start a new diet plan, but after a few days give in to temptations? Make new goals for the future but nothing ever comes of them? Find yourself in a guilt-fuelled rut, which seems to never end? Maybe you read some really good books on personal development and decided you were going to take control of your life, take full responsibility and lead the life you desired and deserved ... Only to find yourself back where you started, feeling worse because you couldn't stick with it?

When we decide we want change in our lives – **positive change** – we get motivated (full of energy) and we can do anything. We feel positive, alive and we even feel that we are serious about doing it this time. It's great when this happens, and often at the beginning of a new year. We know this is the right time to make positive changes and this will be our year.

Nothing will stop me this time – bring on day one! I'll start next week. I'll pay the full year's subscription for the gym, so I'll have to go for the year. Great idea!

Three weeks later:

> ***I can't make it this week – too busy at work.***
>
> ***I'll grab a sandwich here as I've no lunch with me.***
>
> ***Put two sugars in that coffee – I'll be training later and I'll burn it off.***
>
> ***I can't get up at 6 a.m. – I need the lie-in.***
>
> ***I rushed out the door this morning – forgot my lunch and training gear.***
>
> ***I'll do it when I get home – I'll have time then.***
>
> ***It's so hard working with all these negative people.***
>
> ***I seem to be making the same mistakes over and over again.***
>
> ***All this work is starting to pile up and get on top of me.***

Why do we start off so well and then it all fades away and we are back at square one?

I'm going to throw some words at you. Throughout this book you will learn about all these and much more:

- Willpower
- Discipline
- Focus
- Motivation
- Positive attitude
- Visualisation

- Goals
- Actions/reactions
- Reflection/debrief
- Beliefs
- Core values
- Life balance
- Clarity
- Journey/process
- Life's purpose
- Self-love
- Priorities
- Gratitude

If you are serious about making a positive change in your life, then by the time you are finished reading this book, you will be a more motivated, disciplined, focused and positive person. You see, it's very simple: it's your life, you are in control and you need to take full responsibility for it.

I am responsible for my own life.

I am responsible for my own life.

I am responsible for my own life.

No more excuses. No more playing the blame game.

Reality check: you know this is different. Something inside feels different. No more going around in circles, or getting down in yourself over the way your life is, your diet, your fitness, your relationships, your work ...

It's time to wake up.

It's time to make some positive changes.

It's time to take your life back.

It's time to love yourself, life and everything in it.

It's time to take action.

> *I can change a man's battery and then recharge it again. But it is only when he has his own generator that we can talk about motivation. He then needs no outside stimulation. He wants to to do it.*
>
> *Frederick Herzberg*

The day-to-day Positive Living Model is designed for people who want to make a serious effort to make positive changes in their lives. The model is designed for you to:

- Plan your every day
- Stay focused and motivated, every day
- Be in the correct mental and physical state, every day
- Achieve your long and short-term goals
- Be confident in everything you do, every day
- Find a life balance (work, life, recreation, family, relationships, etc.)

Tips for Success

Holistic view

I recommend you take a holistic view of the whole process. By this, I mean that if you are thinking of starting physical exercise, eating healthily, taking up yoga or meditation, etc., then you start with this programme. This will ensure maximum benefit and greatly help you with focus, motivation and life balance. These are very important.

5-to-2 rule

I also recommend that you adhere to the 5-to-2 rule – on Monday to Friday you stick rigidly to the programme in this book but on the weekends you can be more flexible.

Commitment

By giving 100 per cent to this programme, you will achieve extraordinary results in your life. You will be so focused and determined that you will not have to worry about:

- Junk food temptations
- Backing out of exercise sessions
- Giving up on a goal
- Acting negatively to any situation
- Feeling that you are not in control

If you want to get yourself into such a good mental and physical state that you can achieve anything you put your mind to, well, the Positive Living Model is for you.

You don't have to be great to start, but you have to start to be great.

Are You Ready to Set Sail?

Think of yourself as a ship tied up in a harbour, the harbour being your comfort zone. Safe and sound. No stress or hassle. You just sit there all day and watch other ships come and go on their adventures. You hear all the tales of strange places, foreign people and exciting experiences. Your life revolves around what other ships are doing. You admire the other ships.

You sometimes ask yourself, could that be me? Could I venture out into the world and explore life beyond the harbour? What would happen to me if I sailed out to sea ... what would I learn about myself? Could I be like the other ships? Am I good enough?

There is a saying: 'A ship is safe in the harbour, but that's not what it was built for.'

You may be safe living within your comfort zone in life, but you need to ask yourself one question: when your life comes to an end, do you want to be the ship that never left the harbour, or the ship that sailed out into the ocean and discovered the world?

When a ship is about to leave port it flies a flag called the Blue Peter. This is the nautical flag that tells everyone the boat is setting sail. In life, you need to decide whether or not to raise your Blue Peter, set out and be the person you were born to be?

Do not go to your grave with regrets ,raise your flag and set out, explore, learn, live.

Chapter 3
The Daily Action Plan

> *A mind that is stretched by a new experience can never go back to its old dimensions.*
>
> *Oliver Wendell Holmes Jr*

To help us live the Positive Living Model we use our Daily Action Plan.

The Daily Action Plan is broken down into **six parts.** In later chapters, I will go through each part in detail so that you fully understand the importance of each and get the maximum benefit from your plan. In Chapter 17, Putting It All Together, you will learn how to use your plan every morning.

The six parts of the Daily Action Plan are:

- Wake-up
- The mind
- The body
- Actions
- Reactions
- Reflections

Each part is an intricate piece of your Daily Action Plan. This plan will give a complete structure to your day and put you in the captain's role of your own ship. No more being a passenger or spectator in your own life.

I believe every person should live his or her life in the present, not in the past or in the future. There is no point being worried about the past or nervous about the future. Just be happy in the now.

We will look at making goals for the future and working through a process for fulfilling them. But the main emphasis is on a Daily Action Plan that will let you live according to your beliefs and your core values, not anybody else's.

Taking Action

Each day is a precious.

Treat every day like a blank canvas. Create something special.

Each day is a gift.

When your eyes open in the morning and you can see the world, congratulations; You have been gifted another day on this planet.

Each day is priceless.

You can't go back. Each day is unique. Look back on it with satisfaction.

Each day is sacred.

Be the best person you can be. In the mystery of life, we owe that to the creator.

Putting everything into perspective;

What would you do if you were given 3 weeks left to live?

- Would you get up early every day and make the most of the time you had.
- Would you watch all those soaps or get out for a run or walk in nature.
- Would you do some good deeds? Help others.
- Would You get excited if you were stuff in traffic or just realise it's nothing to sweat about.
- Would you worry about going out in the rain or cherish each moment and wish you had never taken the little things in life for granted.
- Would you visit all your loved one's. Would you now find the time in your life to do that?

- Would you reflect back on your days? With regret? Or with satisfaction?
- Would everything in your life be put into perspective?

We don't know how long we are here. Each day is ours to do what we want. You need to decide what's important in your life. Only you can decide this.

People talk about becoming wealthy, of making their fortune, of being able to pay off their mortgage and then, finally, being free. So many self-help books talk about making money and being successful. We are drawn into this 'dreamland' of seeking a life that will completely transform our very being – a transformation that will turn our ordinary lives into extraordinary ones – but very few find the lives they seek. The rest keep moving. Their day will probably never arrive. They seek something in the future, but that's all they do ... seek. There is no plan. No action. It's all wishful thinking. And the worst part is that their days go by one by one, and so too do their weeks, months and years.

We can wish for a lot of things, but if we never take action, we are destined to live our lives in the same way.

Then there is the other side of the coin. There are those who believe that this is their lot and that's that. No point in trying to change it.

> ***This is the hand I've been dealt and I just need to get on with it.***

Either way, instead of wishing for something to happen, or deciding this is all you're getting, why not make the most of every day? Why not treat every day with the respect it deserves? When we live in the now, we make the most of every day, we enrich our lives, we stoke the fires of our souls.

If you're not happy with your normal everyday life, isn't it time to make some positive changes? Isn't it time to live the life you were born to live – you only get one shot at it, so why not give it the best shot you have? What is the harm in eating healthy food, doing some physical exercise, getting your confidence levels up, looking after yourself and looking and feeling great? What's the worst that could happen? You live a happier life?

Gratitude: My Double-H Theory

Healthy = **H**appy

If you enjoy good health, you should have a reasonable level of happiness – fact!

If you are having a bad day, week, month, life but you have your health, you need to go back to your default setting: a basic level of happiness. Because no matter how bad you think you have it, there are millions of people around the world who would love to be able to do what you do:

- Walk in the woods
- See leaves fall from the trees
- Hear the birds sing
- Feel the rain on your face
- Touch the soil

- See the ocean
- Run
- Write
- Read a book
- Smell the flowers
- Drink a cup of coffee
- Hug your children
- Walk your dog
- Breathe unaided

So if you think you're having a bad day because your coffee is too hot, you put a dent in your car or your boss got mad at you, go back to your default setting and take a reality check. You are so blessed with everything you have; you just need to realise it. Take stock, express gratitude, smile. You have no reason not to be happy. You have the mental and physical capabilities to set new goals and then to go ahead and achieve them. Every day when you wake up and open your eyes, you have been given the chance to do whatever it is you want. The world is there for the taking. Every day is a gift to you; make of it what you will. Millions and millions of humans around the globe are not in the position you are in.

This should be enough to motivate you to achieve your goals.

Rethink Success

Success isn't about being rich or having a huge house and fancy car. Success is about you living every day in accordance with your authentic self. Success is about being happy. You will be successful when you wake up and realise that you have been given the gift of life. You are successful when you live every day doing the things you love.

Success starts inside you; it's not something external.

Success starts when you open your eyes first thing in the morning.

Success doesn't choose you; **you chose success**.

Success isn't measured by money or position.

Success is measured by happiness and living a balanced, authentic life.

Do you think all wealthy people are happy? That all wealthy people are living an authentic live? That all wealthy people are happy in their own skin?

I've read a lot of self-help and personal development books and so many talk about success, but they imply that success is about money and position in life. Why do we think that if we are wealthy, we are successful? Does that mean that, if you are not wealthy, you are not a successful person?

What does success look like to you?

If you live every day to the best of your ability;

If you let yourself be happy every day;

If you give yourself permission to live in the now, not in the past or in the future;

If you are grateful for all the wonderful people in your life;

If you achieve a few small goals every day;

If you put your head on your pillow every night knowing you gave the day your best shot;

Are you not a successful person?

It is my belief that you are. You are far more successful than the person with loads of money and a big job who doesn't get to live an enriched, happy, authentic life – a person who misses out on the most important things in life:

- Spending quality time with their family
- Looking after their mental and physical health
- Living each day being happy and content, instead of being stressed and overwhelmed
- Enjoying the beautiful things in life, nature and the outdoors

Some of the happiest people on the planet are those with little or nothing.

The more you want, the more money you need. The more money you need, the more stress you bring on yourself. It's a vicious circle.

People in our society are educated, work and retire. We talk about retirement as if it's then, and only then, that we can really live our lives. What an awful thought. Retirement shouldn't be a target in the future for when you decide to do all the things you want to do –a time in the future when all your troubles will be gone and you'll be happy.

Your future is today!

When you wake up, your future is the next 24 hours. What will you do with it?

You can live a life constantly talking about what you will do, in the future, years from now. Or, you can decide to live your life now.

- Start your garden now – plant those seeds
- Start writing that book now
- Put on your exercise gear and get out there now
- Clean out the junk food in your kitchen cupboards now
- Realise how lucky you are

Nobody knows what's going to happen tomorrow. Take every day as it comes. Make the most of it. When you put your head on your pillow tonight, have no regrets.

You are a successful, happy and enriched person ... if you choose to be. It's up to you.

I am responsible for my own life.

Rethink Obstacles

Your health is your wealth. If you are not in good health, does that mean you should be unhappy? No.

This is an opportunity to gain clarity and put everything in perspective. See this as a time in your life where **gratitude** isn't just something you practise in the morning as part of your Daily Action Plan: it's an in-your-face reality.

Life isn't fair, but if we can see obstacles as opportunities, you can grow to be a positive, successful person. Learn from everything life puts in front of you. It's your choice whether to curl up in a ball and give up or to stand up toe to toe with your realities.

It's at these times that you need to look at the person in the mirror. Take a good look at yourself and look beyond the clothes you are wearing. What are you going to do today? Remember to take each day one at a time. Your obstacles are your opportunities and your opportunities help you to grow.

In survival training, the instructors talk about the psychology of survival. During some survival experiences, people with survival training have perished and died, while others with no survival training have survived. Why is it that this could happen?

It's the **will to live.**

Some people give up, others take the attitude that they are not going to allow the situation to get the better of them and do everything in their power to help themselves.

Anyone can have this kind of mental attitude,if they so wish.

You don't need to wait to be in a survival situation to put yourself into this state. You can do this right now. You can do this every day when you decide:

- To control your emotions
- To be positive

- To see obstacles as opportunities
- That you are not happy with the life you are living
- That you are willing to change the life you are living

Each part is an intricate piece of your Daily Action Plan. This plan will give a complete structure to your day and put you in the captain's role of your own ship. No more being a passenger or spectator in your own life.

By following the **Positive Living Model**, you can create a sustainable lifestyle that will let you live a healthier, enriched, happier life.

> *To the barefoot man, happiness is a pair of shoes. To the man with old shoes, it's a pair of new shoes. To the man with new shoes, it's more-stylish shoes. And of course, the fellow with no feet would be happy to be barefoot. Measure your life by what you have, not by what you don't.*
>
> *Michael Josephson*

Each new day brings hope, opportunity and potential. What you do with it is entirely up to you. You can pull the duvet over your head and surrender your right to live to your full potential. Or, you can jump out of bed and make this day yours.

Chapter 4
The Awakening

> *Fear not that your life shall come to an end but rather i*
> *never have a beginning.*
>
> *Cardinal John Henry Newman*

My Story

I awoke as usual ... but not as usual.

Something was wrong. I felt worried and very down. I ra
brain trying to figure out why I was feeling like as I did but
find the answer. I got up and went about my normal
activities. That whole day I felt down and it started to wc
had never felt like that before.

That night I went for a walk to try to work it out. I walked around and around for about three hours. It was Hallowe'en and the kids were preparing bonfires. I didn't take much notice as my mind was speeding and I was trying to catch up with it, to ask what the problem was and what the bloody rush was.

I remember stopping in the middle of the road and simply saying to myself, 'I'm leaving my job and heading off to Australia.' Just like that.

In that single moment something amazing happened: I started to laugh out loud. There, in the middle of the road, I stood laughing at myself. Everything that had been troubling me just lifted off my shoulders and disappeared; like a flick of a switch, it was all over.

Looking back shortly afterwards, I realised what had happened. Years and years of living a life that wasn't in line with my values and beliefs had finally caught up with me ... I couldn't run away anymore.

For years I had worked in the army – a job I'd dreamed of since childhood. But as with all jobs, it was a case of the grass is greener on the other side. The years leading up to this event were pretty normal. What I hadn't realised was that I was slowly letting myself slip into the same old routine as so many other people. I was:

- Going to work with no real drive, no passion
- Using excuses for everything
- Putting in just enough effort to get by
- Using negative talk so much that it became normalised

- Talking about people behind their backs as if it were the only way to pass the time
- Eating unhealthy food
- Drinking plenty of beer at the weekends
- Doing the bare minimum exercise

I blamed my job for everything. I blamed it because it didn't give me what I wanted when I wanted it. Then I blamed it for giving me what I wanted when it didn't suit me. I wished the days and weeks to pass just so it meant I was finished whatever it was I was doing--I was wishing my life away.

Slowly, over the years it was eating away at me. The life I was living was not in line with everything I believed in. It was only a matter of time before something would break.

I took a career break from the army (following some good advice I received), sold my house and car and gave away a lot of my belongings. It felt great: I was really doing it. I felt so alive and just wanted to spread my wings and live life as it was meant to be lived.

Over the next two and a half years, I travelled and worked in Australia and Africa. My time in Australia proved to be the most rewarding of my life. I trained as an outdoor instructor with Outward Bound Australia. The place, people and the learning will remain with me until I die. When I came home to the army I went to Chad in Africa. What a beautiful place! It is hard to describe--imagine showing a local child their face in a digital camera and the child not knowing who it is because they have no mirrors.

As the next few years passed, I was a lot happier with life. But nevertheless there was something missing. I still felt I was just moving forward without any real direction. I was going through the motions.

Then four days after I got married, something else hit me. This time I didn't see it coming. **I got serious about my life.** I made a decision to take full responsibility for my life. This time I wouldn't blame anyone else for anything that happened in *my* life. No more wishing I could eat healthier and train every day. No more listening to negative chat. I would pull myself back from getting involved in negative conversations. I would take full control over my actions and inactions.

What I'm basically saying is: 'I got my shit together.'

Getting Back to Basics

No secret, no magic. What I came up with was based on good old common sense. Going back to basics. What really amazes me is that we all know 100 per cent what is best for us as individuals – we all know this, but most of us fail to act on it.

> ***Who is in control of my life?***
>
> ***Who is responsible for my life?***
>
> ***I am.***

Do you ever feel that you are just going through the motions, being led along, doing as you are supposed to do? We are born, educated, work, retire ... and then die.

When we are born we have a few years before we go to school. Here we are 'educated', not in matters of life or even how to preserve it, but educated so we can get a job and work. You work until you retire and then with your pension you can do all the things you wanted to do. After that, you die.

Is that what you really want from life? Or is it time to:

- Make every day count?
- Become that confident person you want to be?
- Look at yourself in the mirror and smile?
- Feel full of energy and passion?
- Become the person you were born to be?

Take action now!

This is your time. This is the moment when you realise that you are going to make your life your number one priority.

I'm not saying it's going to be easy: it's going to take a lot of effort. You will have to break some old habits and start new ones, but by doing it on a daily basis, step by step, you *will* succeed. And in the end, you will be amazed with the results.

Work Life

Since we spend a lot of our life at work, I think it's critical to our very being that we enjoy it. We should be excited by it, jump out of bed and actually look forward to it. For many this is not the case. I know it may not be possible for everyone to down tools and leave their jobs for something else, but you don't have to something that drastic in order to improve your work life. Think back – why did you choose your particular job in the first place? Ask yourself what has changed in the years you've been in the job?

Example

I joined the army because I was mad into all the army stuff as a kid. I loved the uniforms, weapons, training, equipment, adventure, travelling abroad, teamwork, challenges, etc. As I got older, these very opportunities were still available to me. However, my attitude gradually changed and a time came in my career when I needed a break. I left for 18 months and, to be honest, it was bloody hard to go back. As the years went by, I felt that the army wasn't for me anymore and so I hatched plans for an exit strategy.

The strange thing is, when I ask myself if the same opportunities for happiness and enjoyment are still available in my current position as when I first joined, the answer is yes. So, why is it I have such a negative opinion of my job? The job itself is pretty much the same: I can still do most of the things in the army as when I first joined. So if the job hasn't changed, it must be me. My attitude has changed and not necessarily the job.

Sometimes the grass is always greener on the other side. We forget about the good things that are available to us at work. It's a bit like how people talk about all the good things that other countries have but fail to mention all the great things we have in our own country. Or, all the things that are bad in other countries.

As with our own lives, we need to take stock of all the good things we experience in our job. Be grateful for them. If we think about the reasons we chose the job in the first place, and if those reasons are still valid, well maybe we need to look at why our attitude towards work has changed.

For me, I firmly believed it was the job. I believed I needed to get out. The job was starting to get so negative I was looking at every option to leave and find something else.

But if I knew back then what I know now, things would be a whole lot different. It wasn't the job: it was me.

Benefits of the Positive Living Model

By following the Positive Living Model you will discover how to live every day to your full potential – how to live a healthier and happier life. Everything will be oriented so you get the maximum out of every day. As I said, there is no secret or magic, just common sense.

Follow the Positive Living Model and start living each day using your Daily Action Plan and soon you will be able to:

- Take your life back and be who you want to be
- Recognise that you need to change your life and gain the moral courage to do it
- Look up to the person in the mirror, and not to someone else
- See your own faults and failings

- Change your mental and physical being so you can actually love yourself
- Place yourself in a positive environment
- Be happy in all aspects of your life

What is the biggest investment you will make in your life? Your home, car, property, shares, etc.? No! The biggest investment you make is the one where you invest in **yourself** – both mentally and physically.

Chapter 5
The Wake Up

Early to bed and early to rise makes a man healthy, wealthy and wise.

Benjamin Franklin

Every day, think as you wake up, 'Today I am fortunate to have woken up. I am alive, I have a precious human life, I am not going to waste it. I am going to use all my energies to develop myself, to expand my heart out to others, to achieve enlightenment for the benefit of all beings. I am going to have kind thoughts towards others. I am not going to get angry or think badly about others. I am going to benefit others as much as I can.'

The Dalai Lama

The first part of the Positive Living Model is to get up early.

'Why?' I hear you ask. Well, that's a fair question. The benefits of rising early include:

- Gaining the time required to implement the Positive Living Model
- Time for yourself (to read or write a book, as I did)
- Time for a healthy breakfast
- No rushing around

- Plenty of time to commute to work
- Productivity – you are more productive in the morning
- Time to do some physical exercise
- No distractions
- Time for personal growth
- Time to meditate
- Visualisation

You can greet the sunrise with a smile or stumble into the day late. For me, I like to greet the day ready and eager.

Positive Living Model Step 1
Make rising early a habit

There are different ways to approach getting up early. I recommend getting up at 06.00 hrs. Personally, this gives me one and a half hours before I leave for work. If you aren't leaving to go to work, for whatever reason, I still recommend you get up early to gain all the benefits from it.

Decide how much time you need in the morning. This can be your first big decision. I recommend one and a half hours before you leave your house.

Some people start by getting out of bed a half hour early and work up to the one and a half hours ... sorry, that's not for me! Set the alarm for 06.00 hrs and when it goes off, get out of bed. It's that simple. Get into this habit and nothing else. If you're serious about making positive changes, then this is what you will do.

After just one day implementing this aspect of the Positive Living Model, you will realise the benefits of rising early.

The good news is that you can decide to do the 5-to-2 model, which is very simple – Monday to Friday you get up at 06.00 hrs and on the weekends you can decide to sleep a bit longer. But remember, you must still adhere to the model whenever you do get up. It may be the weekend but you want to get the most out of it.

If you so wish, you can do the 6-to-1 or even a 7-to-7 model. I prefer the 5-to-2 one. I'm a huge fan of rewarding great work. Put the effort in during the week ... and enjoy the weekends.

'I don't have the willpower to do that.'

Let's look at this statement. What is willpower? Google it:

> *'Self-discipline-training and control of oneself and one's conduct, usually for personal improvement.'*
>
> *'The strength of will to carry out one's decisions, wishes, or plans.'*

If you want to live a life that is far healthier, productive, focused, motivated, balanced, rewarding and happier, I'm 100 per cent confident you will find the discipline to get up at 06.00 hrs in the morning. Because that's what it is: discipline.

Remember, who is in control of your life?

I am responsible for my own life.

We will be touching on motivation later, but if you are still finding it hard to get your head around getting up early or the Positive Living Model in general, let's look at the alternative to getting up early. Does any of it sound familiar?

Example: Getting up on time

Wake up with just enough time to grab a coffee. Rush out the door. Drive to work under a bit of pressure to give yourself five minutes to spare when you get there. The slow driver in front is driving you mad. Try to overtake? Bit dangerous but, feck it, go for it. Get into work ... alive. Underpants intact. You just know it's going to be one of those days.

Example: Getting up late

Sleep in. Get into work late and apologise. At coffee break, grab a sandwich and a bag of crisps and, ah feck it, a chocolate bar – you missed breakfast. Plan on going for a run on your lunch break but your gear bag is at home. You'll do your exercise later if you feel up to it. Grab a coffee on the way home and a small bar of chocolate – need the sugar buzz to keep you going. You wish you could be more disciplined and organised. You hate this feeling of always being rushed and under pressure. Glass of wine when you get back might do the trick ...

Now, find the positives in the above scenarios. If this is how you live your life, all the time or even some of the time, wouldn't it be great to change it to something like this:

Example: Getting up early

> *Get up at 06.00 hrs. Do 30 press-ups and 30 sit-ups. Make yourself coffee and sit down on your favourite chair. Go through your Daily Action Plan: 1. Mental, 2. Physical, 3. Actions, 4. Reactions. Prepare and eat a healthy breakfast. Pack your car with all your work stuff, exercise gear, healthy lunch and a bottle of water. All good. Cleaned up and all ready to go.*

In the last example, you are focused, motivated, disciplined and ready for the day ahead. You won't find yourself deciding over a bag of crisps or chocolate at coffee break; you will have brought your own healthy snack. No mental torture, no temptations. If you want to stick to a healthy plan or physical fitness plan, it's easy. ... yes, I said easy.

You just need to structure your day.

People use every excuse under the sun. Why? Because they have no control over what is happening to them. They give away their control over their lives to chance. When you don't plan your day, give yourself time, organise your stuff and prepare mentally for the day, you give up your control.

Think of all those people you look up to.

> ***Oh, I wish I could be like them, eat healthily like them, train every day like them. How do they do it? Where do they get the time to be so organised and look so professional?***

The answer is probably they:

- Got out of bed early
- Ate a good healthy breakfast
- Prepared for their day – mentally and physically
- Were focused and motivated for the day when they left their house
- Paid attention to detail
- Greeted the sunrise with a smile and an attitude of 'This is going to be a great day'

There is no secret ... no magic. Just plain old common sense.

We all know we should eat healthily, train a few times a week, look after ourselves mentally and physically, etc., but we still do the opposite. Mad, isn't it? We know what we should be doing to live a great, healthy, successful, fulfilling life. But we fall short. We take the easy road, which turns out to be the long bumpy road ... to nowhere worth going.

I decided to listen to my inner self. I decided enough was enough. It was time to get serious about things. So I took my life back.

The old saying 'One life, live it' makes a lot of sense to me. So enough about talking the talk ... it's time to walk the talk.

Remember, motivation is about moving towards something. Every day you wake up you should be moving towards achieving something. Making those positive changes in your life. Moving towards a healthy body and mind. Being confident, every day.

Getting up early will be a challenge. Some will find it harder than others. If you consider getting up early as a mini goal, you will have accomplished your first goal by putting your two feet on the ground every morning.

As the mornings go by, you'll see the benefits. You will realise that you can control your day. Putting structure on your day may be a huge change for you, but it will be the first step in taking control of your life.

Imagine knowing you will eat a healthy breakfast, have the time to prepare and enjoy it. Knowing that you are ready for work, snacks and lunch packed. Imagine, as you sit in your car or on the bus in the morning, that you are mentally focused and motivated to face the world. Knowing you will react in a positive way to what life throws at you.

Just as eating one healthy meal won't make you instantly healthy or eating one unhealthy meal won't instantly make you fat, getting up early once or twice will not create a habit of it for you: it takes work, hard work. But if you decide to go to bed early so you can rise early, well then, you can face the day with the determination and mindset to let you live an authentic life.

You owe that to yourself.

Chapter 6
The Mind

> *'Tis the mind that makes the body rich.*
>
> *William Shakespeare*

Good morning!

So, after getting out of bed straight after your alarm goes off, find yourself somewhere comfortable to sit – in your favourite chair, at your desk (but do not turn on your computer or any other distractions). Have a cup of coffee or tea if you want, and make yourself comfortable. It's time to get your mind in the right mood for the day.

(Note: you can do your morning physical exercise before or after this.)

Gratitude

We now start off the day with gratitude.

Gratitude is being grateful for what you have. Every time we express our gratitude for something (health, family, car, house, cup of coffee, book collection, etc.) we are putting ourselves into a positive frame of mind. We acknowledge all the people and things in our life. We acknowledge how lucky we are right now. All too often we complain about all the things we don't have, which makes us feel empty and down.

Every morning go through everything you are grateful for, especially all the things that are important to you. List it out loud or just in your head.

I am grateful for …

Realise how good your life is at present. How rich it is.

It doesn't matter how much money you have, if you are in ill health; the person with no money but who is healthy is in a far better place than you.

Express your gratitude every morning.

Remember the double-H: 'health' and 'happiness'.

If you have your health, you should have a good level of happiness. So many people are affected by ill health for whatever reason. When you can get out of bed in the morning and are physically and mentally in good shape, you should be happy. You have so much to be grateful for. You are in a position that so many millions around the world would love to be in. Don't waste this gift. Live every day.

By practising gratitude you are acknowledging that you are grateful for being the captain of your own ship. You are aware that you have endless opportunities, which a lot of people do not have. You are grateful for being able to set sail every day into a new dawn, to experience, see, feel, smell, touch and communicate with the universe.

Visualisation

Once you have listed and thought about all you are grateful for, you can move on to visualising your day ahead.

For visualisation, you need to be present; you need to be in the moment. You must focus on what you are doing. Don't let your mind wander. This will help you to get the best results from visualisation.

Use your diary or a notebook and write down everything you need to do during your day. Now, visualise yourself doing all you've written down. In your mind, see yourself completing each task. Not alone that, but see yourself doing everything successfully.

Today is going to be a great day. You are putting yourself in a positive and focused mindset. You will have a successful and rewarding day. Visualise yourself going to work. Arriving at work, what's the first thing you will do? Visualise yourself working. Visualise your break. You are eating the healthy snack you brought. Same at lunch. Visualise your whole day. While doing this it will also trigger thoughts of things you need to organise for work or that you need to bring with you. It's like a little reminder of all the things you need for the day.

Now at this stage you have put structure on your day. You know exactly what you will be doing. You have seen yourself successfully completing everything.

If, for example, you had written 'physical exercise' on your list, you will have visualised yourself in exercise gear and doing that 5K.

You will have visualised yourself finishing the run and feeling the satisfaction of doing so.

If you ever look at some people praying, especially when saying the rosary, you see people who are so-called praying. But to me, they're not. They are simply reciting a load of words. They know the words off by heart and are just rattling them off. It's so bad that people start their part of the prayer before the others have finished theirs. This to me is not praying. To pray you need to be present. You need to know what you are saying. Not alone that, you need to understand everything you say.

Affirmations

Affirmations are a positive-thinking technique for change.

Affirmations are short, powerful statements. When you say them, think them or even hear them, they become the thoughts that create your reality.

You can create any affirmations you want. They are about you and you only. For example:

- I am lean, fit and healthy
- I am a successful and professional doctor
- I am a skilful and talented soccer player
- I am grateful for everything in my life
- I am healthy and happy right now

When you say your affirmations, do so numerous times a day. Each time you do, repeat the affirmation at least 20 times. After a while you can choose to say as many as you see fit.

You have now placed yourself in a positive, motivated and focused mindset. Use affirmations throughout the day to help you. This mindset will see you face off any temptations or anything that will try to derail you from succeeding. You are in control. You are responsible for your own life.

I am responsible for my own life.

Integrity

The carpenter's house

An elderly carpenter was ready to retire. He told his employer of his plans to leave the house-building business and live a more leisurely life with his wife and enjoy his extended family. He would miss the pay cheque, but he needed to retire. They could get by. The contractor was sorry to see his good worker go and asked if he could build just one more house as a personal favour. The carpenter said yes, but in time it was easy to see that his heart was not in his work. He resorted to shoddy workmanship and used inferior materials. It was an unfortunate way to end his career.

When the carpenter finished his work, his employer came to inspect the house and handed him the front-door key. 'This is your house.' he said. 'It is my gift to you.' What a shock! What a shame! If he had only known he was building his own house, he would have done it all so differently. Now he had to live in the home he had built none too well.

So it is with us. We build our lives in a distracted way, reacting rather than acting, willing to put up less than the best. At important points, we do not give the job our best effort. Then with a shock we look at the situation we have created and find that we are now living in the house we have built. If we had realised earlier, we would have done it differently.

Think of yourself as the carpenter. Think about your house. Each day you hammer a nail, place a board, or erect a wall. Build wisely. It is the only life you will ever build. Even if you live it for only one day more, that day deserves to be lived graciously and with dignity. The plaque on the wall says, 'Life is a do-it-yourself project.' Your life tomorrow will be the result of your attitudes and the choices you make today.

Positive Living Model Step 2 Practise gratitude, visualisation, positive affirmations and integrity

Remember;

Your mind is a sacred place. Be very selective who and what you let in.

Visualise this, you are looking at face book and there is a clip of a guy throwing a dog off a large building. The dog falls to his death...

How does this make you feel?

Sickened?

Listening to the news, reading the newspapers and looking at social media can put you in a very negative place. Limit your time in each case. Each day is too important to be going around in a negative mood. Stay positive. Surround yourself with positive people. Listen and read only to positive things. Negative things in life have a way of finding each one of us; we don't need to go looking for them.

I Am Responsible For My Own Life

Chapter 7
The Body

Your body doesn't define you. It's a suit you wear, just like an astronauts. At the same time, it's your suit and you wear it for *life!* You only get issued with one.

Morning Exercise

Try to do some form of physical exercise after you get out of bed – be it 20 jumping jacks and 20 sit-ups, push-ups or something like the yoga pose, sun salutation. Basically anything physical that will get the heart going. You don't need to go into a full exercise session if you don't want to; you can factor in your physical exercise for some time later in the day.

A Healthy and Balanced Diet

Eating healthily is an expensive way to eat.

No, it is not!

When you eat healthily, you may spend more on groceries, but by doing so you put yourself into a certain frame of mind: I am a healthy eater. By following the Positive Living Model on a day-to-day basis, you will no longer be stopping off for those lattes, chocolate bars or sandwiches. The money you will save by not buying junk and reactive food ('forgot my lunch') will balance the books, so no excuses about healthy living being more expensive.

And anyway, wouldn't it be better to spend extra money on keeping your suit in tip-top shape, inside and out. Just like the sports car. Fail to look after it and your vehicle will eventually run low, lose its power. And so will your confidence. And in the end, it will cost you a lot more to try and fix it.

Maybe we should stop asking why real food is so expensive, and start asking why processed food is so cheap.

Breakfast

Eat a healthy breakfast. Take your time – you have time! – and prepare a good, tasty, healthy breakfast.

We all *know* we are supposed to eat breakfast, but let's look at *why*.

- Breakfast is the most important meal of the day. It provides you with the energy and nutrients that lead to increased concentration throughout the day
- Studies show that breakfast can be important in maintaining a healthy body weight
- Hunger can set in long before lunchtime, but because it's not convenient to eat healthily, many people who skip breakfast snack on foods high in fat and sugar
- People who skip breakfast are unlikely to make up their daily requirement for some vitamins and minerals, which a simple breakfast would have provided
- Breakfast provides energy for the activities during the morning and helps to prevent that mid-morning slump

No more excuses! Because you now get up earlier, you have time,reasons and you have the willpower.

Coffee break

Prepare a healthy snack for your mid-morning coffee break. Eating crisps, buns or scones every day with your coffee is going to make you feel guilty and will eat away at your willpower. This is no longer a problem, because from now on you are going to eat a healthy snack instead. You see, you are now prepared; you are no longer reacting to a situation. No excuses. Prepare a healthy snack, bring it with you and in your new mindset you will not want any of that junk. This is the new you!

Lunch

Next up is your lunch. Again, you will have prepared a healthy meal. Every person should choose his/her own healthy food. If you are unsure what 'healthy' entails then ask someone who knows or look it up – there is so much information available out there. If you're still unsure, seek advice from a professional.

If you were to take anything from this book, take this advice: eat healthily.

Eating healthily will help you feel great. No bloating or lethargy. No sweating after a feed of junk, stretched out on the coach like a dead dog.

Not alone will your skin improve ... but so will your self-confidence. And I'm not talking about months here. After only a few days you will see and feel the benefits of a healthy diet. A positive mind and a healthy body. You will be unstoppable.

'Don't focus on losing weight, focus on being healthy.'

Regular Exercise

We all know that if we want to be fit and healthy, we need to eat healthy food and also do some form of physical exercise. We all know this – I've never met anyone who debates this or says it's not true. It's common sense, right?

But yet there are those of us that exercise only to counteract all the unhealthy food we eat. Think about this for a moment. Common sense screams at us to have a look at what we are eating. What would happen if we actually ate a healthy diet *and* did some physical exercise every day?

80/20 rule

There is a rule of thumb called the 80/20 rule. This states that 80 per cent of weight loss is achieved by diet and 20 per cent by exercise. Now, if you are exercising only to keep your weight down and not following a healthy diet, you are fighting a losing battle. On the flip side, following a healthy diet by itself and cutting out physical exercise is also not a wise option. You need to do both. Regular physical exercise is important for many other reasons apart from weight loss and a healthy body.

Benefits of exercising

- Boosts confidence
- Raises energy levels
- Helps you manage stress
- Helps you sleep better
- Helps you overcome depression
- Boosts your creativity
- Helps you to look better
- Helps you to manage anger
- Can keep you sharp well into old age
- Helps you connect with nature

Now tell me why you wouldn't want to get out there and go for a walk or a jog.

As we get older we start to put on weight. It can get to a stage where you look in the mirror and realise that your belly is getting bigger, your 'chin' is becoming 'chins' and those chicken wings are looking tasty. Panic starts to set in.

> ***I'd better take some drastic action. It's time to buy a pair of runners or a bike ...***

But in reality, the bike stays clean and in the garage. The runners are great for gardening and life goes on. Maybe every now and then you get a run in or a blow out, but it's random stuff. Nothing structured or planned.

So then, let's look at the 80/20 rule. It doesn't have to be adhered to 100 per cent but the concept is worth applying. Let's look at 'John's' lifestyle.

Example

If John has an unhealthy diet, this negatively impacts on the 80 per cent part of having a lean, fit, healthy body. If John exercises, he is working on the 20 per cent part. So in reality, as John puts on weight, he is fighting to lose it with a resource of 20 per cent. His odds are 4/1. It's not very fair, is it? If this were a fight, John would be getting bounced around the place by four opponents.

John realised this and decided to keep his personal training going but he also started on a healthy eating programme. The result ... now John is working on 100 per cent. All the odds are with John. John now has a lean, fit, healthy body.

Why do we exercise just to keep our weight down and continue to eat and drink unhealthily? It's madness! It's a crazy cycle, which in the end is not going to result in a healthy body for the average person.

Now let's compare John with Mary.

Example

Mary eats very healthily. Straight away there's 80 per cent ... Boom, go Mary! She isn't a fan of exercise but does realise the benefits of it. So Mary factors exercise into her daily structure. Mary is very healthy, lean and fit.

So, when you decide to lose the belly or chins, first think about your diet – 80 per cent, people!

Let's get serious. It's common sense: combine the 80 per cent from a healthy diet with the 20 per cent from regular exercise and you are going to be lean, fit and healthy.

I am responsible for my own life.

The Fitness Industry

The fitness industry is huge. Companies in this industry make money when people go to their gyms, buy their designer clothing, and drink and eat their products. They sell *fitness* as a product. They only make money if you buy into the whole idea that if you don't train you will never be a healthy weight. The reality is if you want to lose weight and be the healthy, leaner person you dream of, then eat less. Eat less, eat healthily and exercise and you will be set up for success. You will accomplish your desired goal.

Again, it all boils down to basic common sense.

Be careful when you see advertisements that claim to be the answer to all your health and fitness problems. The truth is, you know the answer already: it's the basic stuff. Eat less and healthily and do some physical exercise every day. Simple.

Me, the Sports Car

Our body is precious. It is our vehicle for awakening. Treat it with care.

The Buddha

Let's look at this picture for a while. It's a piece of beauty ...

When people look at us we want them to take us seriously. We want to have the confidence to look them in the eye and hold a conversation. If you worry about your bulging belly or the sweat in your armpits because you are under pressure walking around doing the shopping, isn't it time you asked yourself: 'Is this affecting my day-to-day confidence?'

If you listen to people who have succeeded in changing their lives by eating healthily and sticking to a physical exercise plan, what is the one thing they mention again and again? Confidence ... they talk about how much confidence they now have.

Consider the high performance sports car in the picture ... it's not *your* car; no it's better than that. **It's you**. You are the driver and the car is your body.

You drive around in this shiny new baby, everybody looking at you, admiring you, wishing they had one. Jealous of you.

Where do you think your confidence levels are at? Sky high, right? Damn right!

But what if after you purchased the car, you didn't look after it. You put cheap, dirty petrol into it trying to save some money. Didn't service it,never changed the tyres,stopped polishing it,let the rubbish build up inside it ...

Now when you drive around, what do people say? 'That's a pity. That was a nice car. Shame the way they didn't look after that car. What a waste of a beautiful high performance vehicle.' And so on. You get what I mean.

Do you think that you still have that air of confidence now, as you drive around? Or maybe you don't drive around much anymore and prefer to park the car somewhere? That is, on the couch ...

Your body doesn't define you. It's a suit you wear, just like an astronaut's. At the same time, it's your suit and you wear it for *life*! You only get issued with one.

The chances are we wouldn't mistreat a high performance sports car ... yet we do it to our bodies. We eat so-called food, processed junk food. Lots of wheat, sugar and processed crap. And then we wonder, why me? Why can't I be lean, mean and confident like the guy in the next office?

Like the car when we stop looking after it, eventually we start losing our shine, shape and ability to run efficiently.

Why should you worry about what other people think or say? Good question. Maybe you shouldn't, unless it affects your personal or professional life. But let's be realistic here. Most of us are affected by how other people see us. It's human nature.

If you want to look lean, fit, healthy and feel confident, you can and should. Not for other people. But for yourself. Remember it's your suit. You have to wear it until you die...

Positive Living Model Step 3
Eat less, eat healthily and exercise

If the mirror reflects the body; does the body reflect the mind?

Chapter 8
Actions

When you're off your feet, dream. When you're on them, take action.

Walk the talk ...

In **Actions**, we do all the things we visualised, planned and prepared for during The Mind stage of the Positive Living Model.

Here are some examples of what you can do:

- Exercise
- Eat healthily
- Be confident in everything I do
- Be productive at work and at home
- Be in control of my actions
- Be responsible for everything I do
- Work on my goals
- Be solution focused
- See obstacles as opportunities
- Be in control of my emotions, not the other way around
- Be positive in all my actions and reactions
- Inspire myself and others
- Do a good deed every day

My actions are my only true belongings. I cannot escape the consequences of my actions. My actions are the ground on which I stand.

Thich Nhat Hanh

It's great when we aspire to big things – being rich, successful, having a big house and a fancy car. There is nothing wrong with these things. But no matter how much money you have, what kind of car you drive or the size of your house, you must be happy in your own skin.

All the material items in the world will not compensate you for not living an authentic life. When we are happy in our own skin, we accept ourselves for who we are.

Remember: when you look in the mirror, you see the clothes *you wear.* These are not you – they don't define you. They don't dictate who you are – they are just clothes you wear every day.

When we accept ourselves, we do so from the inside out.

Because you have decided to make positive changes in your life – eat healthily, exercise, take a positive attitude, set goals, and basically look after yourself mentally and physically – you are going to see amazing changes in your life. You will:

- Feel healthier and look healthier
- Lose weight
- Gain clarity
- Prioritise what is important in your life and not waste time on non-important stuff

- Be more confident
- Shine from the inside out and have a positive glow about you

You need to give yourself permission to do all this. You need to tell yourself that you deserve to shine, to glow, to grow. You desire all this. When you grant yourself permission to 'live', you accept yourself for who you are. Now you will make the biggest change in your life: you will start to love yourself.

Once you accept who you are, realise that it's only a suit you are wearing, that you are in control and decide to take full responsibility for your life, you need to **love yourself!**

The suit you are wearing will change. You will have it tailored by your healthy eating, physical exercise and positive mindset. Each week you will see your new suit taking shape. Each week you will grow stronger, more focused and more driven.

You will wake up to all the distractions, lies, false advertising and misleading information out there. For far too long we have been fed so much crap, mind junk, lies.

The tobacco companies, food companies, drug companies, cosmetics companies, etc. have taken us for a ride for far too long. Now it's time to take control back and decide not to believe their rubbish anymore. Why? Because everything you need to know is called common sense. It's all basic stuff that you know already.

But we thought there was an easy option. We chose to believe the ads and the pictures in the magazines and papers. All this mind junk was being fed to us from an early age. But now that you are taking back control, it doesn't matter. Things are going to change.

You are going to live your deserved authentic life. You are going to shine from the inside out. You are going to love yourself and everyone around you.

This is your life..

Every day strive to be your best. Talk positively about yourself and others and do a good deed every day.

Get up early, put structure on your day and put yourself in a mindset of self-control. You will be able to stay focused and highly motivated because you are prepared, positive and 100 per cent committed to being your authentic self.

Positive Living Model Step 4
Use a Daily Action Plan to stay focused

Daily Action Plan

Create a habit

Every day you wash yourself, brush your teeth, change your clothes, etc. You don't even need to think about it, you just do it. By getting into a habit of doing all the things that you have listed in your Daily Action Plan, you will eventually do it with little effort. It will become a habit. Do it every day. This is what a blank Daily Action Plan looks like.

Note: when using your D.A.P. it is highly recommended you do so in conjunction with your diary. The two go hand in hand. By writing everything down, it will keep you focused and help to hold you accountable for your actions. You can refer back to your D.A.P. and diary time and time again throughout the day.

You can start using it now if you want.

See Chapter 17 for one I filled out as an example.

Day: **Date:** **Location:**

Wake up at:

Wake-up exercise (body):

Gratitude (mind):

Diary/To do (action):

Visualisation (mind):

Affirmations (mind):

Breakfast (body):

Snack (body):

Lunch (body):

Snack (body):

Dinner (body):

Exercise (body):

Goals (action):

One of your goals should be to do one good deed every day.

Reaction:

- Set yourself in a positive mood in the morning
- Choose not to react to any negative situations
- When something negative happens, take a few moments before you react. Then do so in a controlled and professional manner
- Limit your time around negative people
- Don't get drawn into negative conversations
- Remember, you are in control of your emotions

Reflection:

- What worked well for me today?
- What could I have done better?
- Is there anything I am not totally happy about today?
- What did I learn about myself today?
- What would I do differently tomorrow?
- Did I use my time wisely today?
- Am I living in accordance with my values?
- Am I staying on track to achieving my goals?
- What was the most positive thing I can take from today?

Or you might prefer this layout:

Daily Action Plan

Day: **Date:** **Location:**

Wake up at:

Mind:

- Gratitude:
- Visualisation:
- Affirmations:

Body:

- Morning exercise:
- Daily exercise – what will you do? And at what time of the day will you do it?
- Breakfast:
- Snack:
- Lunch:
- Snack:
- Dinner:
- Sleep:

Action

- Fill out your diary/to do list for today
- Carry out everything you put in your DAP

- Always working towards my goals
- Refer back to your diary time and time again, so you can stay on track of everything you have to do. As time goes on it will become a habit
- Good deed

Reaction

- Set yourself in a positive mood in the morning
- Choose not to react to any negative situations
- When something negative happens, take a few moments before you react. Then do so in a controlled and professional manner
- Limit your time around negative people
- Don't get drawn into negative conversations
- Remember that you are in control of your emotions

Reflection

- What worked well for me today?
- What could I have done better?
- Is there anything I am not totally happy about today?
- What did I learn about myself today?
- What would I do differently tomorrow?
- Did I use my time wisely today?
- Am I living in accordance with my values?

- Am I staying on track to achieving my goals?
- What was the most positive thing I can take from today?

Note of good deeds.

When I first started out using my daily action plan, the one thing that I found I was failing to do every day was a good deed. When I actually thought about it, there are so many ways in which we can do good deeds. Here are just a few.

- Donate unwanted items to a charity shop
- Visit a friend or neighbour
- Pick up some rubbish
- Cut down on paper use
- Donate blood
- Be positive around people, smile more
- Buy a coffee for a homeless person
- Hold the door open for someone
- Say hello to someone you don't normally talk to
- Offer to help a friend

There are millions of ways to do a good deed. You just need to do at least one every day. Some days you will do more. It's mostly free and it's something that you will enjoy doing.

Chapter 9
Reactions

> *Life is like a grindstone. Whether it grinds you down or polishes you up depends on the stuff you are made of.*
>
> *Anonymous*

In this chapter we will look at what I mean by 'reactions'.

What happens when things don't go according to plan?

- How to respond to all the negative stuff that can happen during the day
- Dealing with negative people
- Understanding and managing the saboteur (the voice in your head)

Every day you see it. You are driving to work and someone pulls out in front of another car – horns start blowing, certain hand gestures are made, you can see the person shouting at the other driver. And then it's all over and life goes on. All parties involved eventually calm down. We react to certain situations without thinking; it just happens.

But what if we planned **not** to react like this? What if we planned to stay calm? How would this change your day? Would you feel better? Would this make your day more positive and productive?

Life will throw a lot of stuff in your direction. Some of it will be serious and warrant a lot of your attention, and some will be of very little significance. The old saying 'Don't sweat the small stuff' holds true. Getting yourself in a fluster will only put you in a negative place. Don't let the small stuff do that to you. The small stuff will appear many times throughout your day. If every time it pops up you react to it, you are going to let all these events take control of your day. You will let these events put you in a place where you don't need to be. Remember, you are in control of your feelings, not the other way around. **You need to manage your feelings.**

There will be times in your life when you will have to deal with events that are more significant. This is when you will need to be fully focused. It will take time for you to understand and come to grips with such an event. They can't be just brushed off; they need to be dealt with. That's just life.

But those small, insignificant events are the ones we can let go. We can simple say: No, I am not going to let something like this have a negative effect on me.

So, in the morning when you are planning your day, under the 'Reactions' heading, you will mentally plan not to react to any of these small, insignificant events.

Negative People

If you want to succeed in business, you surround yourself with highly motivated, professional and positive people. If you want to succeed in life, you should surround yourself with ...?

Take a moment to think about it: whom do you currently surround yourself with?

Do these people have a positive or negative effect on your life? At your place of work, it can be very hard to *not* be around people who are negative. They have a special way of sucking the life out of everything. Even in your large group of friends you will find someone who is less than positive.

> *Negative people need drama like oxygen. Stay positive, it will take their breath away.*
>
> *Anonymous*

If you want to succeed in life, you need to be around family and friends who are there to help you grow as a person. Help you become the person you desire to be. Your family and friends will encourage you to push yourself outside your comfort zone. They are there to support you.

Negative people only bring you down. They scrape away at your motivation. They drain you of your positive energy. So how do you deal with this problem? You can:

- Become aware of them
- Avoid them, or if you can't then limit your time in their company
- Let them live in their world if that is what they want
- Choose to live in your own drama-free world – one where you choose to be positive, free and alive

Life is far too short to live every day in a TV drama soap.

Like successful business people, if you want to live a successful life, you need to surround yourself with positive people. Think positive. Be positive.

The Saboteur

How do you react to the voice in your head? You know that voice ... it pops up from time to time. Sometimes it says something that gets your attention:

- You're too fat
- You're not good looking
- You're not good enough
- You'll never be successful

This voice, this saboteur, works away in the back of your head trying to influence you into doing what it wants. It is more than happy to keep things the way they are. It doesn't like change. It will eat way at your willpower and take little bits of truth and turn them into a big lie so you don't make any changes. Don't feed this saboteur by giving it the time of day.

Once you are aware of this internal saboteur, you can choose to override what it is saying. So when you start your positive living Daily Action Plan, it's going to start chatting: **ignore it!**

I once did a parachute jump. Now I'm not great at heights, so this was a bit of a challenge for me. It was a static line jump. This meant I had to climb out on the wing of a small single engine plane and hang on to the bar underneath the wing. The instructor would then give me the thumbs up and I had to let go. The parachute was attached to the plane, so all I had to do was hang on. The chute would pull open by itself ... happy days.

Right, so during training for the jump, the instructor was going through all the actions. We had to go through the drills as well and shout everything out. At one stage she stopped and asked me if I was in the army. I said, 'Yes, why?' She replied that it was the way I shouted everything out with confidence. She then told everyone to do the same. Before we boarded the plane, she asked would I jump first as she wanted someone with plenty of confidence to do it. I'm not a good actor so I don't know how she didn't realise I was dreading the jump. However, I said, 'Yes, thanks for asking me.' So, as the door opened and I looked out into the clouds and at the ground way down below, I nearly died. The voice in my head was screaming at me: 'You are going to die – this is suicide ...'

But the funny thing is I wanted to opt out from doing the jump, but I was too embarrassed to say it to the female instructor ... mad or what? The voice in the head was telling me I was going to die, but I was more worried about the embarrassment of not jumping.

I jumped or, more like, let go ... It was one of the most amazing experiences I've ever had. I loved it. That feeling of floating down towards the earth was incredible.

So the point of the story is I ignored the voice in my head. Even though it was telling me I was going to die. The embarrassment issue aside, I believed in the training I had just received, I believed in the instructor and I believed that my parachute would work.

You can always ignore that voice in your head. Just let it go ...

I have found it very handy to have a mini version of my Daily Action Plan at hand at all times. When those occasions arise where I may be tempted to stray off track or I listen to my saboteur, I take out my DAP and read it. I use it to refocus and stay on track. You may have daily goals, like eating a well-balanced diet today, but that voice in your head is telling you how nice it would be to have a large latte and chocolate bun right now ... your goal is your goal. Ignore the voice! You will feel much better for it afterwards.

Now let's look at your belief system. If you do listen to the voice in your head, you will have formed a negative opinion about yourself. Don't let that voice make you believe you are not good enough. Remember, your attitude and actions come from what you believe. You must be positive and ignore any self-limiting beliefs.

See Chapter 15, **Beliefs,** for more.

Making any kind of change in your life can be a challenge. Making *positive* change needs effort. It needs action. It requires you to stand up and say that this is the right time. This is your life and you are going to live the best life you can.

Control Your Emotions

The problem is it is not that easy. So what can we do to help ourselves?

We are emotionally led beings. We react to our emotions. We can do this without stopping and thinking about what it is we are about to do.

> ***I think I'll skip training – I just don't feel the love for it today.***
>
> ***I'd love a burger and chips – it's just so convenient.***
>
> ***I'd love to have everything my neighbour has.***
>
> ***Every time I talk to him, I get into a heated argument.***

We react to our emotions and do things that we later regret. If this is the case, why not knock it on its head. Before you do something emotionally led, stop and ask yourself this question: **What way will I feel after I do this?**

The chances are you will feel pretty bad about yourself for eating that junk food, not going for that run, getting into a heated argument or being envious of other people.

So, stop, think and ask yourself that question. Don't be led by emotions: use your head, your brain. Remember, you manage your emotions; your emotions should not manage you.

Now ask yourself: what way will I feel if I stay strong and do what is best for me?

This is definitely going to make you feel better about yourself. Another little victory. Achieving another daily goal, one at a time.

> *When dealing with people, remember that you are not dealing with creatures of logic, but creatures of emotion.*
>
> *Dale Carnegie*

Set Boundaries

Learn to say no. Ask yourself, is it in my best interest? If not, say no. Some people can't say no – they put everyone else ahead of themselves and don't look after themselves enough. This is not good for you.

You need to ignore that voice in your head telling you to do all those things for everyone else. You can't do everything for everyone. Eventually you will pay the price for it. Then you are no good to yourself or anyone else. Look after yourself first. Your family and friends want you to be at your best. Ignore that voice in your head – it doesn't like change.

Plan Your Reactions

When you are filling out your Daily Action Plan, in the Reactions section list the challenges you may face in the day ahead. Take note of how you will react when faced with these little challenges. Remember, every time you ignore the voice in your head, you are winning a small victory. And when you are reflecting on your day, you need to acknowledge this. All these are small steps to you living your authentic life.

Remember: **today + today + today = success**.

Meaning, all the small things you do every day will lead you to success. It's very important that you realise this. It's not about having one great day and six bad days – strive to do your best *every day*. All the small things add up.

Positive Living Model Step 5
Choose to react to negative situations
by 'not reacting'
and do not be led by your emotions

Chapter 10
Reflections

What I hear I forget. What I see I remember. What I do I know.
Chinese proverb

Every day we wash ourselves. We shave or take off our make-up. We change our clothes. We brush our teeth. We basically cleanse ourselves of the grime and dirt from the day we have just lived.

We are very good at cleaning our 'suit'... but how do we clean our inner self?

- How do we clean off all the negativity and grime we have accumulated from our day?
- How do we learn from our mistakes?
- How do we process what we have learnt about ourselves?
- How do we debrief our day so we can transfer everything we have learnt and use it the following day?

We need to reflect.

Every day we go through many experiences. It can be hard to learn from these experiences right away. When we reflect back on how we dealt with different situations and experiences, we can learn so much about ourselves. From this learning we can develop into the person we want to be.

If we don't take time to reflect each day, we risk the missed opportunity of learning from our experiences. This can lead to making the same mistakes again and again.

Methods of Reflecting

There are many ways of reflecting. Find a nice quiet corner in your house. Pick your favourite chair. Grab a cup of tea and pen and paper.

Keep a journal

Before going to bed every night, write down in a journal how your day went. Write about your experiences, fitness regime, healthy eating, what you learnt about yourself, tips you picked up, etc.

When you write something down it helps to clarify it. You can go back and look at it in the future. When you see it written down you will be forced to think about it. This thinking/reflecting will help you to develop into a person who values learning from their life experiences.

Reflection isn't just about looking back at *negative* things that have happened. Reflection also involves thinking about *everything* that has happened – look back at all the good things you did, your exercise, your healthy eating, your good deeds, etc. Acknowledge that you are focused and disciplined in your life.

Go for a walk

Take time out in the evening for a walk. Walking is a great way to spend time reflecting on your day. While out walking (which has many obvious benefits), you will be able to put everything into perspective and it will set you up nicely for the following day.

Talk to someone

It's good to talk. Have a chat with someone – perhaps with your partner, a trusted friend or a family member. Discuss your day.

Another option is to engage with a **life coach**. A life coach will champion your success as much as you do. They will ask you smart questions that will make you think about your life. Working with a life coach can be done on a monthly basis or whenever you want. There are many ways in which a life coach can help you. If you decide to use one, my advice is to ring them first and discuss in detail what you want. Life coaches should tell you if you are both suited for working together and if you aren't then they may recommend you seek help from another more suitable coach.

Whatever way you decide to 'reflect', don't underestimate the importance of taking time out at the end of each day for reflection.

Tips for Reflecting

To help with your reflection time, you can ask yourselves some questions. But not any old questions: **smart** questions. Smart questions are the ones that get you thinking about yourself. They're the ones that take a few minutes or more to answer.

- What worked well for me today?
- What could I have done better?
- Is there anything I am not totally happy about today?
- What did I learn about myself today?
- What would I do differently tomorrow?
- Did I use my time wisely today?
- Am I living in accordance with my values?
- Am I staying on track to achieving my goals?
- What was the most positive thing I can take from today?

You can create your own question list. By doing this every day you work on the cumulative effect of being a better person.

Positive Living Model Step 6
Take time to reflect

Chapter 11

Your Well-Being

You want to be happy in your life?

Put everything into perspective. Keep it simple. Stop pursuing happiness, pursue to be happier. Stop looking for something that you already have. You can be happy now. If you so choose.

Do you ever feel that you can't function correctly, are overwhelmed, stressed out or even depressed?

You don't need to be a doctor to realise that all of the above will have a negative effect on you, both mentally and physically.

When we lose control of our lives and don't manage our time correctly, we are going to make ourselves ill. We start to feel overwhelmed and stressed out. Everything begins to get on top of us. It's hard to focus on any one thing as there is too much going on in our lives. This can have a negative effect on our home lives and how we interact with other people, especially those who are important to us.

So, when we have more time, we are more productive. When we have less time, we are less productive.

Having time for family and friends is an important aspect of living authentic lives. Family matters, our friends matter. Running around chasing our tails, with stuff that probably isn't as important as family and friends, is not going to help us live fulfilled lives.

The Importance of Balance

We all need to live balanced lives. There is no point in having a great job and making loads of money and then coming home late, wrecked, tired and fit for nothing. A balanced life is where you have balance across the board. It's so important that we all take action to ensure we find this balance in all areas:

- Family and friends
- Work
- Social
- Health
- Fitness
- Spiritual
- Personal growth
- Fun and recreation

It's about quality and not quantity. When we fail to find balance in our lives, we leave the door open for problems. The person who knows you best is you. Every now and again we need to check in with ourselves and take stock on how we are doing – gain some clarity in our lives. If something isn't right, we need to stop and fix it. Don't just plough on and hope for the best. Take action. (This is covered in Chapter 16 **The Wheel of Life**.)

The first step is to acknowledge you aren't living the life you desire. After that you need to determine what exactly it is that you want, what positive changes you want to make so you can live a better, more positive and fulfilling life.

You need to set a goal. (This is covered in Chapter 12 **Goal Setting**.)

Listening to Your Body

Do you listen to your body? What do you do when you have a headache, feel bloated, lethargic, have a bad back, inflammation, a rash, pain in your feet, depression, etc.?

You go to the doctor, you get medicine. A pill for every ill.

Do you ever stop and think that maybe, just maybe:

Your headache is due to dehydration? Do you drink too much coffee and not enough water?

Your rash is due to your bad diet? Are you eating enough fruit and vegetables?

The inflammation is from too much dairy or wheat in your diet?

Or,

If you are depressed because you are overweight ...

If you are depressed because you are so unfit ...

If you are depressed because you have no energy ...

It's not the depression that's the problem ... it's being overweight. It's your body telling you, quite loudly, that you are overweight and you are killing yourself, that you need to take action and you need to do something right now.

When we fail to listen to our bodies, then our bodies will have to take action.

Let's take exercise as an example. When you don't exercise, you might as well take a depressant. Your body, mentally and physically, isn't built for sitting down all day: it needs exercise. This is basic stuff. You don't need to be a doctor. You just need to listen to your body.

Now as I'm not a doctor, I can't say what exactly you should be doing, but I can recommend a few things. As a life coach, I recommend you do the following for an optimum sense of well-being:

- Put structure into your day (Positive Living Model)
- Educate yourself on health and fitness (read books, watch documentaries, etc.)
- Do regular physical activity
- Live a balanced life (see Chapter 16 The Wheel of Life)
- Eat a healthy diet
- Drink plenty of water
- Be grateful
- Love yourself
- Live each day
- Learn from your mistakes
- Forgive
- Set realistic goals
- Take action

Don't wait until it's too late: take action today. Take control of your life today.

We spend so much money on our houses, cars and material things but not on what really matters. Our health matters. It's not too expensive to eat healthily. You would spend it on a big car or new clothes but not in the 'suit' you were put in, for the rest of your life.

We need to prioritise what is important to us. Having all these material things is great, but if we are overweight, stressed, unfit, unhealthy and have no time in our lives, well then they are no good to us anyway.

Spend your money on your health and well-being – on improving the quality of your life.

Invest in yourself

Nowhere in this world will you get a better return on your money than by spending it on your quality of life ... it's basic common sense.

Listen to your body; don't ignore it. If you do, you will pay a great deal more in the long run.

Take responsibility.

I am responsible for my own life, not your doctor or any other healthcare professional. You are responsible. They can recommend to you what is best, but it's you that needs to take action. You can't blame them if you don't look after yourself. You need to take personal responsibility.

> *Be yourself, but always your better self.*
>
> *Karl G. Maeser*

Chapter 12
Goal Setting

The greatest danger for most of us is not that our aim is too high and we miss it, but that it is too low and we reach it.
Michelangelo Buonarroti

When you decide to set yourself a goal, or goals, you enter into a process that has a beginning, a journey and a finish.

Your starting point is where you are now. Your journey is the route you decide to get to the finish (the process). The finish is where you accomplish your goal.

Some examples of goal ideas people may have:

- To get promoted to line manager
- To run a 10K race
- To lose X amount of weight
- To find a new job in a certain field
- To find a partner
- To bench press 140 kg
- To give up smoking

These would not be considered full goals: they are the basis for a goal – the starting idea.

No matter what your goal is, you must be serious about achieving it. Also, you must take on the whole process with a 'can do' mindset.

Before you start you need to look at a few things that will give you maximum advantage.

For setting goals, I use the GROW VERY SMART model:

G.R.O.W.

Goal/**R**eality/**O**ptions/**W**ill

V.E.R.Y.

Vision/**E**motions/**R**esponsibility/**Y**ours

S.M.A.R.T.

Specific/**M**easurable/**A**ttainable/**R**ealistic/**T**ime Based

G.R.O.W. G = Goal

What is your goal?

G.R.O.W. R = Reality

Where are you now? What is your **current** reality?

Before you plan a journey route, you need to know where you are starting from. This gives you vital information about the best route to take.

Example

Your goal is to get promoted to line manager in 12 months, but you ***currently*** *do not have the required skills for the job. So you know that in your current situation you will not succeed in your goal. You now have 12 months in which to up-skill.*

G.R.O.W. O = Options

What do you need to do right now to get you on your way?

If there are any obstacles, how will you negotiate them?

Are you in this on your own, or do you have help?

Do you need to do some research?

Do you need advice?

Do you need to educate yourself?

There will be many options you can choose to move forward with. Take your time. Find the best one for you. If you're not sure about something, ask someone.

G.R.O.W. W = Will

On a scale of 1 to 10, rate how serious you are about achieving your goal? If it's not 10 out of 10, you will have significant difficulty in succeeding. If it's only a 5, you will not achieve your goal.

Go back and read all of the above.

V.E.R.Y. V = Values/Vision

Is your goal in line with your values? (see Chapter 14 Values.) When your goal is in line with your values, you will be more motivated to achieve it. This will also bring balance into your life.

Can you visualise yourself achieving your goal? What does it look like?

V.E.R.Y. E = Emotion

Are you excited and energised by the thoughts of achieving your goal? You should be.

V.E.R.Y. R = Responsibility

You are responsible for your own actions and inactions. You must hold yourself accountable.

V.E.R.Y. Y = Yours

Is the goal yours? If not, whose is it? You should only be setting goals for yourself. Check before you start: who am I doing this for?

S.M.A.R.T. S = Specific

What exactly are you trying to achieve? Keep it short and to the point. A big, long-winded description is no good. Keep it specific.

Example

I will run 10K in 44 minutes on the 25th of June.

S.M.A.R.T. M = Measurable

How will I know I have achieved my goal? Be sure you have a clearly defined finish you can recognise once you reach it.

If your goal is to 'run a 10K race', it will be obvious you have achieved your goal when you pass the finish line. If your goal is to 'lose some weight and get a bit fitter', it's going to be harder to tell when you achieve this. Keep it measurable and meaningful. Your goal should be important to you and you should know when you have achieved it.

S.M.A.R.T. A = Attainable

Can I actually do it? If your goal is to 'run a marathon in a week's time' and you haven't trained in five years, then it probably isn't attainable. If, however, you decide to run a marathon one year from today, and put in place a step-by-step training programme, then the chances of achieving your goal will be far greater.

Your goal *must* be attainable or you are setting yourself up for failure.

S.M.A.R.T. R = Realistic

You decide to learn to play a new instrument. You think it would be nice to be able to do it but you're not very excited or motivated about it. Due to time constraints in your daily schedule, you have very little opportunity to practise for a few hours every day.

You need to identify if your goal 'fits' into your life in your current reality. If your goal involves something you're rather indifferent about and 'wouldn't mind doing', you are not going to achieve your so-called goal. You must also take into account how your journey to your goal will fit into your everyday life, and how it will affect your need for a well-balanced life. That is, you want all parts of your life to stay in balance. For example, your goal is to get promoted, which will mean you have to spend more time at work and bring work home with you. If this will have a negative effect on the rest of your life, you must ask yourself if it is a realistic goal.

A well-balanced life is extremely important to your health and well-being, and to your loved ones. Keep it realistic.

S.M.A.R.T. T = Time based

Anchor your goal to a certain time. By doing this, you have a definite date to work towards. The worst thing you can do is to set a goal for some vague time in the 'future'. By anchoring it to a date, you have a start point and a finish point. Now all you need is the step-by-step process for getting there.

Example

I will run a 10K race on the 7th of June this year.

If you set your goal too far into the future, you will need to set mini goals along the way. If you don't, you can easily stray off track and lose focus. To stay highly focused you need to set these mini goals along your journey which will ensure you utilise your time properly.

So let's put it all together: G.R.O.W. V.E.R.Y. S.M.A.R.T.

Example

My Goal is to run a marathon in under 4 hours .

*My current **Reality** is that I haven't done any physical activity in two years (I had a knee operation so running was out of the question). I used to love running every day. It was a way to clear my head and get my thoughts together.*

*My **Options** are to join the local CrossFit or circuit classes. I could also join the running club to get me back into the swing of things. The members of the club would be very supportive and help to get me back to the level of fitness I was at.*

*Yes, the running club is the way to go. That's what I'll do. I'm fully committed to doing it. My **Will** is 10 out of 10 in fact.*

*I can **Visualise** myself crossing the line within my goal time. I see in my mind's eye the delight and sense of accomplishment in myself. Just thinking about it and visualising it gets me **Excited** and **Energised.***

*As part of my daily positive living, I know that this is another **Responsible** decision in living a better and healthier life.*

*This is my goal. I'm doing this for **myself** – (**Yours**). It's something I've wanted to do for a long time. Now is the time.*

Specific

- *My **goal** is to run a marathon in under 4 hours on the 28th of June this year in Dublin city.*

Measurable

- *When I cross the line I will have completed it.*

Attainable

- *I will start today on a training programme*
- *To judge my progress I will set mini goals for the end of every month*
- *I will get advice from friends who have ran marathons*
- *I will start off slow and build up my miles*
- *I'll complement my training with a healthy diet and balanced lifestyle*

Realistic

- *I have the time to train and I'm highly motivated to do it*
- *I'm in pretty good shape and I'm healthy*
- *I've no injuries and a brand new pair of runners in the wardrobe*
- *The training programme fits nicely into my daily routine*

Time

- *I've anchored my goal to a date*
- *I have a year to prepare*
- *I'm running a 10K race in 3 weeks (10.00 hrs on 5th of November)*
- *I'm running a half marathon in 6 months (09.00 hrs on 10th of April)*

A goal without a plan is just a wish.

Antoine de Saint Exupéry

Example

Orienteering is the art of navigation and fitness, and the objective is to correctly run to a certain number of kites (where you punch your card to show you were there) and to do so in the least amount of time. Your equipment is very simple: a map and a compass. If the orienteer were to simply run straight to the finish, they would fail miserably. They would have missed all the kites and the journey would be a complete waste of time.

When setting a goal, you first need to know where you are starting from. The orienteer starts by locating himself on the map: the beginning. He now has a choice on which route he will take to the first kite. The easy route might be longer and the hard route might be shorter. What really matters is that he works within his ability. ***He makes a plan.*** *He will use his compass to point him in the right direction. Likewise, in life, we use our moral compass to point us in the right direction. Our moral compass guides us; it helps us to distinguish between right and wrong.*

When the orienteer gets to the first kite, he punches the card and immediately starts to work on the next piece of navigation. By correctly arriving at the first kite, he now reaffirms he is still on the right track. Because he arrives at the correct kite, he knows he is still travelling in the right direction and this keeps him motivated.

When the orienteer gets to the finish, he punches his card for the last time. As in goal setting, orienteering is an individual effort. You may get help along your journey towards your goal, but the goal itself should be for you. You need to know your starting point, navigate with your moral compass and have mini goals along the way to show you that you're still on track. Staying on track will reaffirm that all your hard work and dedication is paying off.

It's a dream until you write it down, and then it becomes a goal. Make your goals big – dream big! Write them down in a list and put your list where you can see it every day. Visualise yourself having achieved your goal.

When you start out with a new goal, it can be helpful to ask yourself these three questions:

- What must I **start doing** in my life in order to achieve my goal?
- What must I **stop doing** in my life in order to achieve my goal?
- What must I **continue doing** in my life in order to achieve my goal?

Remember, coming up with a goal is only the starting point. You now have to take action. You have to move towards it. Otherwise it will always be in the distance.

Discipline is the bridge between goals and accomplishment.

Jim Rohn

Chapter 13
Motivation

> *If we wait for the moment when everything, absolutely everything, is ready, we shall never begin.*
>
> *Ivan Turgenev*

I worked as an outdoor instructor in Australia from 2007 to 2008. The company I worked for was called Outward Bound Australia. My year with this company was to have a huge positive impact on my life. I remember saying after the year was up, that if I died the next day I could do so with a smile on my face, for I truly lived for the year I was there.

The year with Outward Bound Australia was a rollercoaster ride of emotions. I learnt more about myself and other people in that year. I figured out some of my core values and beliefs. I even changed some of my beliefs. That year had a profound effect on me, one that shaped me into who I am today.

But enough about me; I want to tell you a story about a little girl and motivation. I was an instructor on a 10-day school course in Western Australia. The purpose of the course is to help the kids' personal development. It's an intense course in that the kids stay out in the wilderness for the 10 days. They hike, canoe, climb, cave, cook, navigate, cry, laugh, etc. It's a full-on course that has huge benefits for all involved, including the instructors.

After a long day hiking over sand dunes and some featureless terrain, we came to our camping spot for the night. It had been a long day. The sun was burning and we all appreciated getting into camp.

Everybody started into their assigned jobs. The shelters were put up, food was prepared, wood collected and a fire started. The evening passed off quietly. After dinner we cleaned up and settled in around the fire for the nightly debrief/reflection.

We talked about everything and how things were going, for better or worse. We discussed how we could improve our performance. Kids thanked each other for the help and encouragement they'd received throughout the day. One of the key topics that popped up was motivation. When I asked if anyone had anything to say on it, one girl said she would like to say something. Naturally, I encouraged her to speak and sat back to see what was going to happen.

The girl was about 12 years old, with dreadlocks and braces. She had a pretty, friendly face with a mature smile. She wasn't very tall and, sitting there by the firelight, she looked smaller than usual. But when she spoke, she blew us all away.

'I want to talk about motivation for a minute. I just don't understand what some of you guys are doing. It seems to me that some of you are saving up your motivation, and trying to carry it over into the next day. I don't understand this. It doesn't make sense.

'The way I see it is you get 100 per cent motivation every day. So you use up that 100 per cent on that day. When you get up in the morning, you wake up with 100 per cent motivation in the bank. You are free to use it all that day. Make the most of that day. Don't worry

about tomorrow or the next day – they will come with their own motivation.

'People sitting here around this fire are trying to save a certain percentage of today's motivation and carry it over until tomorrow. So they aren't giving 100 per cent today ... some are only giving 50 per cent and think they can carry over the other 50 per cent to the following day – this doesn't make any sense. Every day you start off with 100 per cent motivation that's yours to use throughout the day. The next day, you get another 100 per cent ... it's that simple. Stay motivated all day – give your best every day. That's all I have to say.'

I was shocked. As I looked around the fire at the other kids and the teacher, I knew I wasn't the only one. I was scribbling it all down into my notebook for future reference and at the same time trying to get my head around what this 12-year-old girl had said. We all sat there for a minute and nobody talked.

I can't quite remember what happened after that but I do know it had a huge effect on the other kids. They all heard what was said and they all acted on it.

I've retold this story many times, especially when team building. I think if a 12-year-old girl from Western Australia can figure this out, we all should be able to.

When I hear people say they don't have enough time to make changes in their lives, or they are not able to stay motivated to complete their goals, I think of this story.

Motivation is like fulfilment and happiness – we actually don't need to be in constant *pursuit* of it. We can be motivated *now*.

We can be happy *now*.

We can be fulfilled *now*.

We can always want to be happier, more fulfilled or even more motivated, but this pursuit (of wanting to be more) should not be the be-all and end-all. If you live in the moment, live for every day. You can decide to be what you want to be ... today.

Wake up with 100 per cent motivation in the bank account. Don't try to carry any over to tomorrow. Use it all up today.

You don't need to find motivation, you already have it. You just need to use it wisely.

Chapter 14
Values

> *Values are not like laws – you cannot break them. You can only break yourself against them.*
>
> *Mark Wright, The Integrity Coach*

I believe that if you want to live an authentic life, you need to know your values in life. If you know your values, you will be far happier, motivated and healthier.

What Are Values?

First, let's look at what values are. Values are intangible. Here are some examples of values:

- Comfort
- Compassion
- Love
- Loyalty
- Support
- Wonder
- Enjoyment
- Kindness
- Integrity
- Independence

- Humour
- Adventure
- Privacy

Hyrum Smith (2001) defines values as 'what we believe to be the greatest importance and highest priority in our lives'.

Some people will say that their values include their family, money, house, car, etc., but these are not values. What these things give you are *values*: love, friendship, security, freedom, etc.

It's hugely important that you know what your values are. To help you identify your values, think of all the times you were really happy.

- What were you doing?
- Who were you with?
- Where were you?

Now look at the values that follow from this.

Another way to help you identify your values is to remember the times you were very cross.

- What caused you to get so mad?
- Who caused you to get mad?
- Where did this happen?

When someone makes you really furious, it may well be that they are stepping on your values. Look at which values they are and use this to find what values you have.

In the book *Emotional Intelligence Coaching*, the authors use the example of a tree. The roots of the tree are the values, beliefs are the trunk, attitudes are the main branches and the leaves are our behaviours and actions.

So our behaviour stems from our attitude, which comes from our belief system, which in turn all starts with our values.

If you know what your values are, you will know what makes you tick. If you are in a job that is not in line with your values, well then, you will not like your job.

If you work with people who step on your values, you will not see eye to eye. While saying that, you need to understand that the other person has their own values, which may differ from yours. You need to realise this and have the emotional intelligence to understand that you in turn may be stepping on their values.

Values and Goal Setting

You should set goals for yourself that are in line with your values. If not, you will find it harder to motivate yourself to achieve your goal. You may even achieve your goal, only to find out that it was not what you wanted after all. All because your goal wasn't in line with your values.

Stephen Covey (1999) talks about people climbing to the top of their ladder, only to find it's leaning up against the wrong wall.

If you want to set yourself up for success, make sure your goals are in line with your values. Think back to when you were doing something you really loved doing. How excited were you? How motivated were you? How full of energy were you?

When you do something that is in line with your values, it becomes the most natural thing in the world. Why? Because you are living an authentic life. You are doing what you are meant to be doing. When you ask yourself what your purpose in life is, the first thing you need to do is to live an authentic one: live a life that is in line with your values.

> ***Example***
>
> *You work in a job based in an office with no windows. You work long hours alone all day every day. Your values include freedom, camaraderie, adventure, flexibility and spontaneity. What are the chances that you hate your job? Understandably so. You are living a life that is against your very being ... this will eventually result in ill health and you living a miserable life.*

Do you know what your values are?

Chapter 15

Beliefs

What you believe today, may cause disbelief tomorrow.

As a child growing up in Ireland, like most I believed 100 per cent in one thing: the Bible. Our religion, our faith, all goes back to this one book. As I grew older I noticed something very peculiar. My belief system on this matter was severely challenged. I believed that all Christian teaching came from the Bible, but yet the Catholic Church was adapting to change in society. So suddenly, hell, fire, everlasting suffering and the devil were talked about less and less. The Old Testament and the **New Testament at times contradicted each other.** So how could I base my belief system on a book that is supposed to be the bedrock of the Christian religion, but which changes to suit modern society and stay in tune with the masses?

How will my belief system look 20 years from now? How can we change what we believe in when the very book we take our teaching from stays the same?

Changing Beliefs

Let's look at it another way. Imagine a man in court charged with murder. A book of evidence has been put together by the prosecution side. Everything in the book points to the defendant being guilty. The jury issue a guilty verdict and the man is sentenced to 25 years in prison for murder. Case closed. Everyone believes 100 per cent that the man deserves his sentence. However, five years later, with the aid of new technology, some of the evidence that helped to convict him is discovered to be false. In fact, it's looking very much as if an innocent man was put in prison.

Now, we believed 100 per cent in the book of evidence five years ago, but now that book doesn't stand up to this new evidence. We could just say that we still believe 100 per cent in the original book and leave the man locked up, refusing to change our belief system.

Or we can acknowledge the fact that we were wrong, we have changed our belief and now believe he is innocent. If we left the man in prison, even though we knew that the original book wasn't as full of facts as we were led to believe, what does that say about us?

All around the world there are people killing, raping, beheading, torturing, robbing, etc., all in the belief that their actions are in the name of their religion. They *believe* they are right and their enemies are wrong. And where do they get all their evidence from ... a book.

Your beliefs will change over time if you open your mind. They say your mind is like a parachute: it works better when it's open.

What you believe now may be different next year. As a child you believed what adults told you (be it good or bad). Over time we change our beliefs – we do this through life experiences, education, travel, meeting people, discussions, debates, looking at TV, reading, etc.

Unlike your values, which remain pretty much unchanged, your beliefs *will* change.

I find it fascinating how we as humans can hold onto our beliefs even though there may be little or no evidence to prove us right. You can call it faith, intuition, gut feeling or whatever you like, but I still like to have some concrete evidence to back it up. Believing in things through blind faith can have a very negative impact on your life if it involves you believing negatively about yourself.

How to Change Negative Beliefs

Do you find yourself saying and believing any of the following?

- I can't do that
- That's not for me
- There is no way in the world I would be able to do that
- I'm not clever enough for that job
- I don't deserve that promotion
- I could never be that fit
- I could never lose the extra weight

Show me the evidence you can't do it ...

Do you have any?

If not, then you need to change these 'self-limiting beliefs' and turn them into 'empowering beliefs'.

> ***Example***
>
> *Instead of:*
>
> *I'm not good enough for that promotion* ***(self-limiting belief).***
>
> *Try:*
>
> *I'm hard working and have lots of experience. I'm more than good enough for that promotion* ***(empowering belief)****.*
>
> ***Example***
>
> *Instead of:*
>
> *I'm too fat to join a CrossFit gym* ***(self-limiting belief).***
>
> *Try:*
>
> *I'm very determined and I've done harder things in my life than this* ***(empowering belief)****.*

When you talk negatively to yourself, ask yourself why you believe what you say to be true. Is there any evidence to back it up? The chances are there aren't any.

Beliefs can be changed; you have the power to change them. Before you believe something to be true, ask for the evidence. If there isn't any ... well, now you need to decide if you believe it or not.

In our modern society we are bombarded with information. The problem is we don't know what's true and what's false because everyone has an angle.

It's the same with all the chatter in your head. If you find yourself saying 'I can't' or 'I'm not good enough', you need to examine this – is there evidence to back it up? If not, you need to change your belief on the matter.

Think positively. Life is too short to have regrets. Push yourself out of your comfort zone; outside your comfort zone is the place where you learn most about yourself.

Don't make your decisions while sitting on the couch – go to that gym, climb that mountain, stand at the starting line, get dressed for the occasion, make that salad for your lunch ....

Believe in yourself. Surround yourself with real friends who truly believe in you.

> *Whether you think you can, or you think you can't, you're right.*
> *Henry Ford*

Chapter 16
The Wheel Of Life

Don't go through life; grow through life.

Eric Butterworth

Do You Have Balance in Your Life?

Using the Wheel of Life to review difference aspects of your life is a great exercise to check if you do have balance in your life. It also gives clarity when setting goals. It's a very individual exercise and you should take your time completing *your* Wheel of Life.

Each segment represents an area in your life. In this exercise you review eight areas in your life. If you wish, you can add or subtract as you see fit. So for instance, you may decide to review four areas in your life, or you may do twelve.

Rate each area out of ten, according to how satisfied you are in that area of your life at this moment in time:

- 0 indicates very dissatisfied
- 10 indicates very satisfied

Here is an example of a completed Wheel of Life.

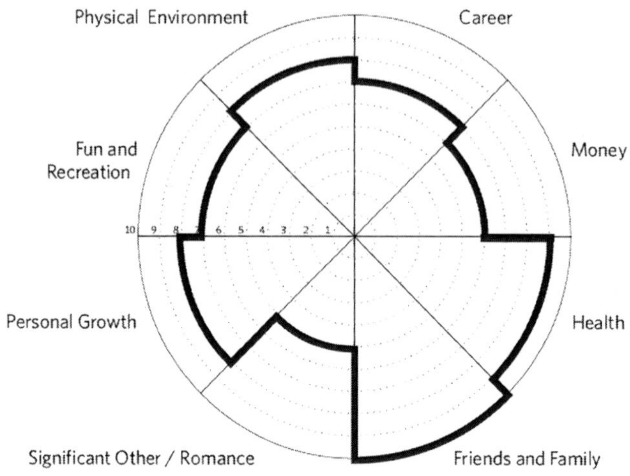

Sample Wheel of Life

You may like to shade in each area.

In the example given, does it look like the person has balance in their life?

The blank Wheel of Life on the next page is for you to fill in.

You can change the areas to suit your own life, for example, if you work full time in the home you might prefer to use 'Home life' instead of 'Career'

Go ahead and fill in the sample to find out how balanced your life is.

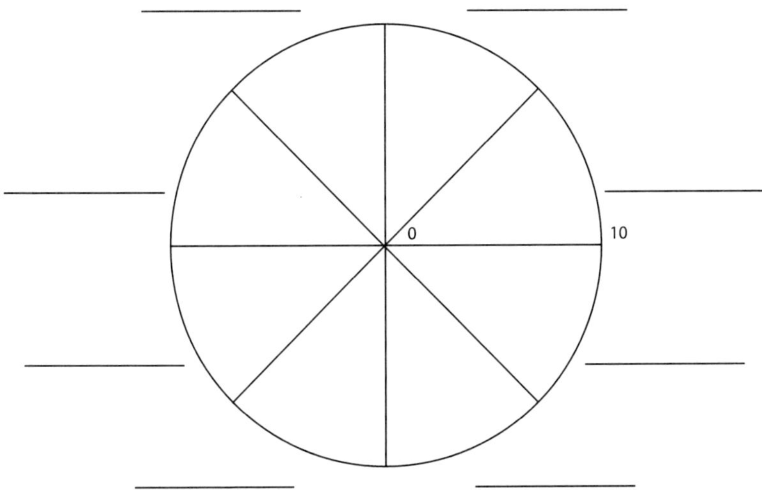

When you are finished, take some time and study it. You can now get a clear view of each area in your life. As you study it, ask yourself these questions:

- Is it balanced?
- Is there anything that really jumps out at you?
- If you were to pick one area to change, which one would you pick?
- How could you get that one closer to 10?

For example, if 'Career' is 5 out of 10, how can you get that to 8 out of 10?

Go through each area and see how you can improve each one.

One of the really significant advantages of using the Wheel of Life is that it helps people to see how unbalanced their lives are.

And if one area is really low, it can have a knock-on effect on other areas. Sometimes people think that a certain area in their life is the problem, where in reality the problem is coming from somewhere else.

> ***Example***
>
> *Say your relationship is not going great. You and your partner argue a lot over certain things. One of those things is your health. You are not looking after yourself. You are not exercising and your eating habits leave a lot to be desired. This will show up on your wheel as low scores in the areas of relationships and health (and potentially other areas), but your problem may lie in the fact that you leave for work early and don't come home until late. You don't give yourself enough time to look after yourself. You also have no time to spend with your loved ones. This is putting a lot of pressure on you and it's affecting your health.*

The Wheel of Life is a great tool for helping you get some perspective on your life. Use it and see how much balance you have in all areas of your life.

This exercise isn't about getting 10 out of 10 in every area: it's about getting *balance* in these areas. There isn't much point in having 10 out of 10 in 'Career' and 'Money' but only 2 out of 10 in 'Relationship' and 'Health'. Something will give and it won't be good for you.

This all goes back to taking responsibility in your own life.

You can use the internet to find plenty of free examples of the Wheel of Life.

Using the Wheel of Life to Set Goals

The Wheel of Life is a great tool for helping you to identify your potential **goals**.

For example, you score 1 out of 10 in 'Health' or 'Fitness', so you may decide to set yourself a goal in this area.

You can refer back to your Wheel of Life time and time again. Every time you do, you can start with scoring for your current situation.

Remember, the question to ask yourself every time is:

How satisfied am I with [chosen area] at this present moment in time?

If your wheel of life gets buckled. Stop and Fix it.

Chapter 17
Putting It All Together

> *Consider the postage stamp. It secures success through its ability to stick to one thing until it gets there.*
>
> *Josh Billings*

Sample Daily Action Plan 1

Day: Monday **Date:** 12th May **Location:** Home

Wake up at:

06.00 hrs

Wake-up exercise (body):

20 push-ups and 20 sit-ups

Gratitude (mind):

I'm grateful for my wife, family, health, friends, home, etc.

(State everything you are most grateful for.)

Diary (action):

Write down your daily plan:

07.15 Take dinner out of the freezer

07.30 Leave for work

09.00 Start work – pack paperwork for morning brief

11.00 Coffee – pack two bananas and an apple

11.20 Physical training session with the troops – pack training gear and rain jacket

13.00 Lunch – pack a chicken salad

14.00 Do my own training – 6K run – double-check that my training gear and a bottle of water are packed

15.00 Lecture – ensure I have my computer and all training material

17.00 Return home

18.30 Dinner and then downtime

Visualisation (mind):

I can see myself doing everything that's in my diary. I go through it and visualise myself completing every task.

Affirmations (mind):

Repeat: 'I am a positive person.'

(This is a very personal thing; choose your own affirmations that are relevant to you.)

Breakfast (body):

Two boiled eggs and porridge

Morning snack (body):

Fruit (packed)

Lunch (body):

Chicken salad (packed)

Afternoon snack (body):

Scone (once or twice a week)

Dinner (body):

Stew from the freezer (pre-cooked at the weekend)

Training (body):

Run 6K at 14.00 hrs

Daily goals (action/reaction):

Stay positive throughout the day

Choose to stay calm in negative situations

Do one good deed today

Knock 30 seconds off my run time

(The run will help me work towards my bigger goal of a sub-45-minute 10K on the 29th of June this year in Cork.)

Reflection:

- **What worked well for me today?** I did everything I said I would do in the diary. The run went well. Work was good and I stuck to my healthy eating plan.

- **What could I have done better?** I could have been better prepared for my lectures. They went well but I could be better. More research needed.
- **Is there anything I am not totally happy about today?** I need to stop being drawn into negative conversations. I must try to be more aware of this.
- **What did I learn about myself today?** I have good communication skills and an ability to get my point across.
- **What would I do differently tomorrow?** Be more positive and stay clear from any negative conversation.
- **Anything else?** I'm now 100 per cent sure I'm addicted to coffee ... ha ha!

Sample Daily Action Plan 2

Here is an alternative format for your Daily Action Plan. I have included some prompts to help you fill it out.

Day: **Date:** **Location:**

Wake up at:

Mind:

- Gratitude:
- Visualisation:
- Affirmations:

Body:

- Morning exercise:
- Daily exercise: [What will you do? At what time of the day will you do it?]
- Breakfast:
- Morning snack:
- Lunch:
- Afternoon snack:
- Dinner:
- Sleep:

Actions:

- [Fill out your diary for today. Do it the night before or on the morning of your DAP.]
- [Carry out everything you put in your DAP.]
- [Always working towards my goals.]
- [Refer back to your DAP regularly so you can stay on track for everything you have to do. As time goes on it will become a habit.]

Reactions:

- [Set yourself in a positive mood in the morning.]
- [Choose not to react immediately to any negative situations.]

- [When something negative happens, wait a few moments to think how best to respond. Respond when you are ready, in a calm and professional manner.]
- [Limit your time around negative people.]
- [Don't get drawn into negative conversations.]
- [Remember, you are in control of your emotions.]

Reflection:

- What worked well for me today?
- What could I have done better?
- Is there anything I am not totally happy about today?
- What did I learn about myself today?
- What would I do differently tomorrow?
- Did I use my time wisely today?
- Am I living in accordance with my values?
- Am I staying on track to achieving my goals?
- What was the most positive thing I can take from today?

Your Daily Action Plan is all yours. You can change it as you see fit. Put in your own questions or arrange it as you like.

You may be wondering about the *daily* goals. I don't use the **GROW VERY SMART** method for my daily goals. These are smaller goals that I set myself to make each day as productive as I can. The **GROW VERY SMART** method is best suited for your big goals in life. Remember, the model is an aid to help you in achieving those big goals, it's not a must do. Use it as you see fit.

Happiness is neither virtue nor pleasure nor this thing nor that but simply growth. We are happy when we are growing.
William Butler Yeats

I'm hoping that at this stage you have enough to start your Daily Action Plans.

I recommend you create a large, detailed Daily Action Plan (A4 size) and a smaller summarised version of it that you can carry around with you for the day. You can refer back to this concise version time and time again, especially at times when you need that little bit of motivation.

Know Your Goal

Before I leave you off to work on your own, you need to ask yourself one important question:

What is your number one goal right now?

If you were to pick one area of your life you want to change, what would it be?

This might help you to identify your goal.

You have been granted one wish. You can wish for anything you want. Now, I'm not talking about money or a flash car here; I'm talking about a wish that will change something in your life in a positive manner. What would it be?

This is your starting point.

Use this as your **goal**. You now need to build a **plan** so you can achieve this. Use the **GROW VERY SMART** method and your **Daily Action Plans**.

Ensure your new goal is in line with your **values**.

When you put structure to your every day, you are following a definite plan, which will lead you to where you want to go.

Ask for Help

Do you need help? If so, just ask. Ask your family, your friends, professionals. People want to help each other. Sometimes it can be hard to ask someone if they need help. It's easier when they ask. So if you need help ... just ask. I've known people in my life that I regret not helping. I could have asked, but I didn't. I really regret this. But if they had asked, I would have helped them out in any way I could. But we live and learn. Every day is a school day.

Whatever you decide to do, surround yourself with like-minded people. By doing this you will get the support from everyone else in the group. You can also support other members. There is no need to pursue a goal on your own.

Feel the Fear and Do It Anyway

Don't put off starting your new life. Don't let fear stand in your way. Remember, we don't **grow** when we are in our comfort zone. We need to challenge ourselves; we need to take that first step. When you decide to do something new and you're afraid of starting, the chances are you are on the right track.

Let me tell you of a time I was terrified of starting something new.

Picture this: I was in a national park in Australia. I was parked in a campervan, which I had bought a few weeks previously, outside Outward Bound Australia's national base, preparing to go in on my first day. Now leading up to this I had sold my house, car and got rid of a lot of my belongings back home. I had invested a lot of money in my new adventure. I had no friends within a few-thousand-mile radius. I sat in my van, in the middle of what I thought was nowhere. I had never felt so lonely and afraid in my whole life. I kept asking myself, 'What am I after doing?'

Now that my goal was staring me in the face, I was nearly in tears. I didn't know anybody. This new environment was completely alien to me. I kept thinking I was out of my depth, that I didn't belong there, that I wouldn't make a good outdoor instructor in Australia. I thought about turning the van around and heading to the capital Canberra to re-assess my plans. Instead I took some deep breaths and drove in through the gate. I repeated to myself, 'This is the plan, stick with it. Trust in yourself. For God's sake, you're not the first Irishman to come to Australia and ask himself what the hell he's doing here.'

That evening I was standing on a small hill looking out on the beautiful Mount Tennent. As I stood there with all the other interns, our instructor Ben told us that the next few months were going to be a rollercoaster ride. We were going to reach great heights and also there would be some lows on our journey.

He didn't lie. It was that: a journey of discovery. I learnt more about myself than I ever had before. I pushed myself outside my comfort zone so many times. I laughed, cried and I wanted for nothing. I slept under the stars in some of the most amazing places around Australia. I met some of the most beautiful people one could ever meet. I experienced living in the natural world for weeks on end. I said far too many goodbyes than I care to remember. But if I was to die tomorrow, I can always say that for one year of my life ... I lived.

Now that might seem strange. But during that year I faced so many fears and overcame them. I learnt so much about myself, other people and the world in general. I did this because I took the road I was terrified of taking ...

Success Bank

When you start off I recommend that you open a **success bank**. This is very simply a record of all your little victories and achievements. Write them down and **review** them at the end of every day/week/month. You will be amazed with everything you have accomplished. This will be great for your **motivation**.

Remember, as regards motivation, you are more likely to be motivated about doing something when you're *actually doing it* compared to before you start. Take going to the gym as an example. You might be talking about it, putting it off and finding excuses about not going today. But when you get there, when you're in your exercise gear and you're actually exercising, you are more motivated to get on with it. You need motivation? Just go and do whatever it is you have planned to do! Add it to your success bank. Another little victory.

Now, I have read a lot of self-help books. One of the major problems I have with them is that they tend to start off well but then start to waffle on. This is my cue to finish up before I start to waffle on for the sake of it.

Life is a journey. Your journey. We all have our own issues and problems we need to sort out. But we can't keep blaming them on our circumstances. We need to have a good look at ourselves and see where it is we need to go.

Take control of your own life. Make a plan. Stick to it. Structure each day and live a life that is authentic and positive. Strive for 10 out of 10. Whatever happens happens. But at least you can say you've done your best. And that's all we can do, our best.

At the end of every day when you put your head on your pillow at night, ask yourself:

Did I give today my best shot?

Whatever your answer is, remember this:

I am responsible for my own life.

All the best,

Fergus

> *In three words, I can sum up everything I've learnt about life: it goes on.*
>
> *Robert Frost*

ACTION

MIND

D.A

WAKE UP

BODY

.P.

REFLECTION

REACTION